Space Encyclopedia

LONDON, NEW YORK,
MELBOURNE, MUNICH, and DELHI

Written and edited by Caroline Bingham

Design team Gemma Fletcher, Poppy Joslin,
Sadie Thomas, Mary Sandberg, and Bookwork

Editorial team Carrie Love, Lorrie Mack,
and Penny Smith

Publishing Manager Susan Leonard
Art Director Rachael Foster
Category Publisher Mary Ling
Picture Researcher Andrea Sadler
DK Picture Library Claire Bowers
and Rose Horridge
Production Editor Jonathan Ward
Production Controller Claire Pearson
Jacket Designer Hedi Gutt
Jacket Editor Mariza O'Keeffe

Consultant Dr Jon Woodcock

First published in Great Britain in 2008.
This edition published in 2012 by
Dorling Kindersley Limited,
80 Strand, London, WC2R 0RL
Penguin Group (UK)

Copyright © 2008 Dorling Kindersley Limited

10 9 8 7 6 5 4 3 2 1
001–DD434–Jan/08

A CIP catalogue record for this book
is available from the British Library.

ISBN 978-1-4093-8117-4

Colour reproduction by MDP, UK
Printed and bound in China by South China Printing Co. Ltd.

Discover more at
www.dk.com

Contents

What is space?

4-5   What is space?
6-7   Where does space begin?
8-9   Stargazers
10-11   Observatories
12-13   Radio telescopes
14-15   Our place in space
16-17   Great galaxies
18-19   The Milky Way
20-21   Nearby stars
22-23   The Universe

Exploring space

24-25   Exploring space
26-27   Astronaut in training
28-29   What's in your suitcase?
30-31   Rockets
32-33   Moon journey (*Apollo 11*)
34-35   Men on the moon

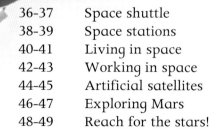

36-37   Space shuttle
38-39   Space stations
40-41   Living in space
42-43   Working in space
44-45   Artificial satellites
46-47   Exploring Mars
48-49   Reach for the stars!

There is a question at the bottom of each page...

The solar system

50-51	The solar system
52-53	The Sun
54-55	Eclipse of the Sun
56-57	Mercury
58-59	The morning star
60-61	Third rock from the Sun
62-63	The moon
64-65	The red planet
66-67	King of the planets
68-69	Jupiter's moons
70-71	Saturn
72-73	Distant twins
74-75	Pluto

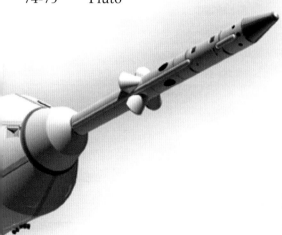

Comets and meteors

76-77	Comets and meteors
78-79	Just passing
80-81	Shooting stars
82-83	The asteroid belt
84-85	Asteroid landing
86-87	Space debris

Mysteries of space

88-89	Mysteries of space
90-91	UFOs
92-93	Is anyone there?
94-95	Is there life on Mars?
96-97	The Big Bang

98-99	Black holes
100-101	Are there other Earths?
102-103	A star is born
104-105	Death of a star

Space for everyone

106-107	Space for everyone
108-109	Become a stargazer
110-111	Phases of the moon
112-113	Constellations
114-115	The northern sky
116-117	The southern sky
118-119	Space technology
120-121	Space timeline

Reference section

122-123	Glossary
124-127	Index
128	Picture credits and acknowledgements

About this book

The pages of this book have special features that will show you how to get your hands on as much information as possible! Look out for these:

The **Curiosity quiz** will get you searching through each section for the answers.

Become an expert tells you where to look for more information on a subject.

Every page is colour-coded to show you which section it is in.

weird but true These buttons give extra weird and wonderful facts.

What is space?

Space holds many secrets. It contains places where human beings can be stretched into spaghetti shapes, or boiled, or frozen solid: that's why astronauts wear protective clothing in space. Welcome to a mysterious – and endlessly fascinating – world.

What is space?

When people think of space, they think of:

 Weightlessness – everything floats as if there's no gravity.

 Nothingness – vast areas of space are completely empty.

 Stars – every star is a burning ball of gas. Our Sun is a star.

 Astronauts – people who explore the world beyond our Earth.

 Rockets and satellites – are what scientists use to explore space.

 Silence – there is no air in space, so there is absolutely no sound.

A nebula is a cloud of dust and gas in space. This is the Helix nebula, about 700 light years away, seen from NASA's *Spitzer* Space telescope.

Is that space?

On a cloudless night, you can see thousands of stars. Space is the name we give to the huge empty areas in between the atmospheres of stars and planets. Apart from the odd rock, space is sprinkled only with dust and gas.

Too big to imagine

Astronomers measure distance in space in light years. One light year is the distance light travels in one year: that's 10 million million km (6 million million miles).

How old is the Universe?

Why is space so dark?
Space is black because there is nothing there to reflect light. From space, Earth looks lit up because light from our Sun reflects off sea, and land, and the particles in our atmosphere.

American astronaut Michael Gernhardt went on four separate space missions, and spent more than 23 hours walking around in space.

Curiosity quiz
Look through the What is space? section and see if you can identify the pictures below.

Become an expert...
on searching for a star, pages **48–49**
on living in space, pages **40–41**

Experts believe it's just under 14 BILLION years old.

Where does space begin?

Earth is cloaked in a thin layer of gases – the atmosphere. Outside this atmosphere is space, where there is no air to breathe, or to allow wings to fly, and where nobody can hear you scream.

Fading away

Our atmosphere does not just end suddenly – it fades gradually into space.

View from *Mir*

Photographed from the American shuttle *Atlantis*, the Russian *Mir* space station once orbited above Earth's atmosphere.

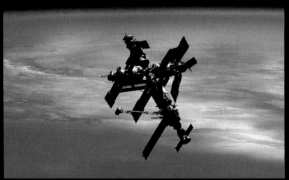

EXOSPHERE

THERMOSPHERE

MESOSPHERE

STRATOSPHERE

TROPOSPHERE

The **exosphere** is the outer layer of the atmosphere, extending about 10,000 km (6,000 miles) above the ground. From here, lighter gases drift into space beyond.

The **thermosphere** reaches way up to more than 700 km (over 400 miles) above Earth. The polar lights (*aurora borealis* in the north and *aurora australis* in the south) glow in the thermosphere.

Most experts agree that space begins at 100 km (63 miles) above the ground. Past this, our image is not drawn to scale.

In turn, the **mesosphere** extends about 85 km (53 miles) above the ground. The air is thin here, but it's still thick enough to slow meteorites down.

The **stratosphere** rises about 50 km (31 miles) above the Earth. Planes cruise in the upper troposphere or lower stratosphere, above the clouds.

The **troposphere** extends between 6 and 20 km (3½–12 miles) above the ground. All our weather takes place in the troposphere.

What do we call the mix of gases that makes up our atmosphere?

Space badge

The American space agency NASA awards astronaut wings to service personnel and civilians who have flown more than 80 km (50 miles) above the Earth's surface. Shown here are civilian astronaut wings.

If you could drive a car straight up, it would take only about an hour to reach space.

Gaia, a European satellite due for launch in 2011.

Slipping through air

A spacecraft has to be streamlined to move easily and safely through air. Where necessary, an extra part called a fairing is added to achieve this effect – a nose cone is a fairing.

The parts of a space shuttle (the orbiter, fuel tank, and rocket boosters) are streamlined for lift-off.

Space hat-ellite

Up in space, satellites can be any shape at all. They don't need to be streamlined, because there's no air there.

Stargazers

People have looked at the night sky for thousands of years. This study is called astronomy. Around 400 years ago, a special tool was invented to make the task easier – this tool is called a telescope.

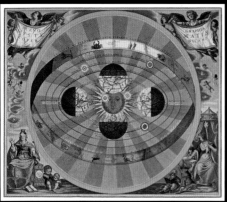

Copernicus placed the Sun at the centre of the planets. He "stopped the Sun and moved the Earth".

Before the telescope

People were shocked when Polish astronomer Nicolaus Copernicus suggested in 1543 that Earth was just another planet and the planets orbited (went around) the Sun. They had believed Earth was at the centre of the Universe.

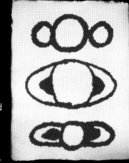

Saturn as sketched by Galileo. He thought Saturn's rings were two moons – or "ears".

Guess what I can see!

The Italian astronomer Galileo Galilei built a simple telescope in 1609 and proved Copernicus had been right. He discovered Venus had phases (like our moon), he saw Jupiter's moons, and he spotted mountains on our moon.

Replica of 17th-century telescope

Saturn as we know it today.

Who invented the first telescope?

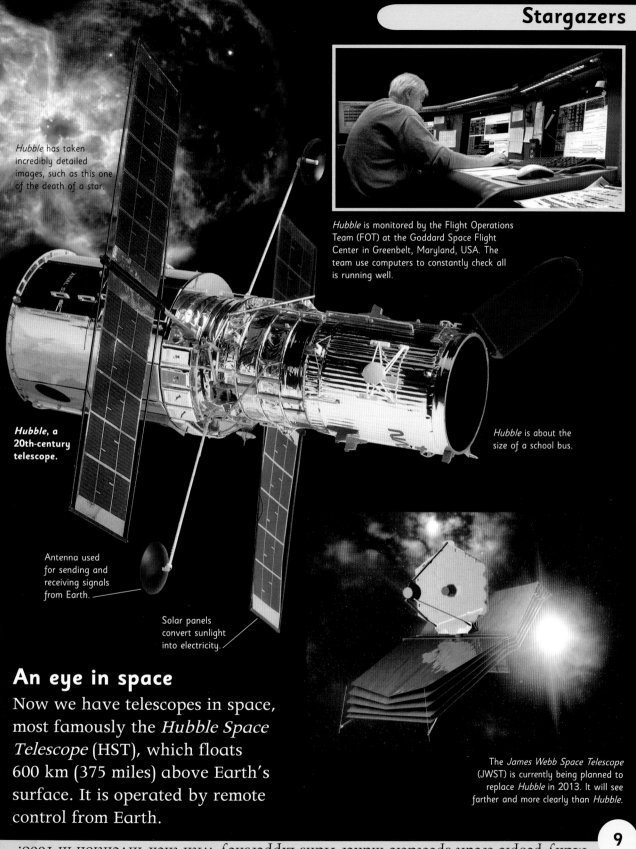

Hubble has taken incredibly detailed images, such as this one of the death of a star.

Hubble is monitored by the Flight Operations Team (FOT) at the Goddard Space Flight Center in Greenbelt, Maryland, USA. The team use computers to constantly check all is running well.

Hubble, a 20th-century telescope.

Hubble is about the size of a school bus.

Antenna used for sending and receiving signals from Earth.

Solar panels convert sunlight into electricity.

An eye in space

Now we have telescopes in space, most famously the *Hubble Space Telescope* (HST), which floats 600 km (375 miles) above Earth's surface. It is operated by remote control from Earth.

The *James Webb Space Telescope* (JWST) is currently being planned to replace *Hubble* in 2013. It will see farther and more clearly than *Hubble*.

Many people credit spectacle-maker Hans Lippershey with their invention in 1608.

Observatories

Light is constantly reaching us from space, and one way astronomers learn about space is by studying this light. To do this effectively, an astronomer needs a telescope and a clear, night sky.

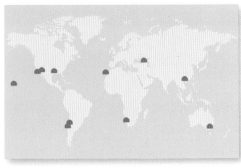

The world's major observatories are all on extinct volcanoes or high mountains, as this is where the air is clearest.

Island observatory

The world's largest light detecting telescopes are the twin Keck telescopes. These are on the summit of Mauna Kea, a dormant (sleeping) volcano in Hawaii. They both contain mirrors that are 10 m (33 ft) across.

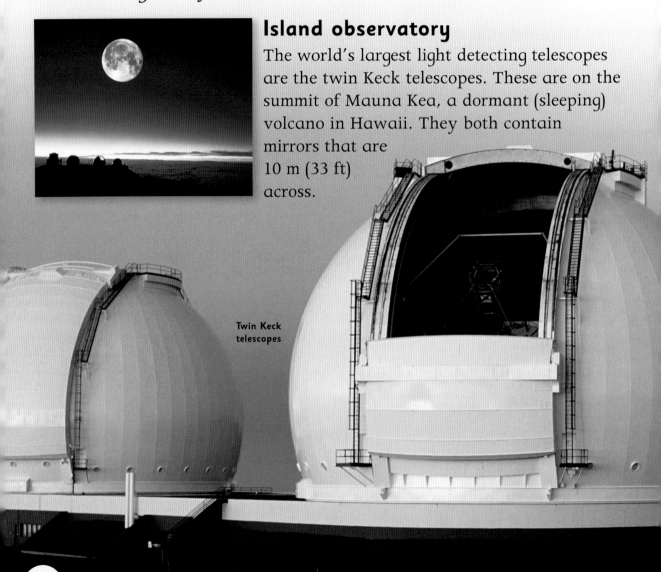

Twin Keck telescopes

From how far away can the *Chandra* spot something as small as a road sign?

A better view

The Royal Greenwich Observatory moved its telescopes three times because pollution clouded their view. Originally in Greenwich, near London, England, the telescopes ended up in the Canary Islands, 2.3 km (1.4 miles) above sea level.

Space telescope

Scientists use the *Chandra* X-ray telescope to study black holes and exploding stars.

A 'Finderscope' is used to line up the main telescope.

What's in a name?

A telescope with a lens or mirror, called an optical telescope, gathers more light than the human eye. Large telescopes use mirrors: the larger the mirror the more it can see. Telescope projects are often given grand names… there's the Very Large Telescope, the Overwhelmingly Large Telescope, and the Extremely Large Telescope.

The summit is clear of light and dust pollution.

Large mirror inside

Near to the twin Keck telescopes are the Canada-France-Hawaii Telescope and Gemini North.

From up to 20 km (12 miles)

Radio telescopes

How a radio telescope works

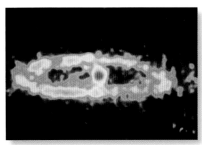

Incoming radio waves

Dish

Aerial

Radio waves reflect off the dish and focus at the aerial.

Receivers amplify and detect radio signals.

Invisible radio waves surround us. They also reach us from space, and large dishes are used to pick them up, day and night, to help astronomers learn more about space.

So do the dishes "listen" to space?

No. Radio astronomers do not listen to noises. Sound waves do not pass through space. The dishes pick up radio waves, a receiver measures them, and a computer turns this information into a picture.

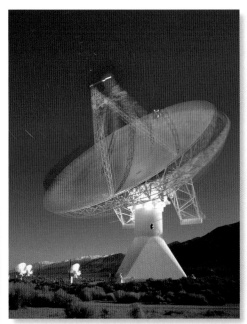

Radio telescope image of the Andromeda Galaxy. The red centre is producing the strongest signals.

Tilt and learn

Radio dishes are designed to tilt and move around, so radio astronomers can point them at the bit of space they want to study. Also, as the Earth turns, radio dishes need to move in order to follow one spot in the sky. The movements, which are controlled by computer, are very precise.

No mountain in sight!

Unlike optical telescopes, radio telescopes don't need to be built at the top of mountains, as radio waves will pass through cloud cover. Each dish reflects and focuses the incoming radio signals onto an aerial mounted above it. The dishes can be enormous.

Can you name some of the everyday uses of radio waves, apart from for radios?

Big in every way

The Very Large Array (VLA) in New Mexico has 27 dishes, each 25 m (82 ft) in diameter. Used individually or together to sweep the sky for signals, they rest on tracks and can be spread over 36 km (22 miles)!

Astronomers didn't discover radio waves from space until 1932.

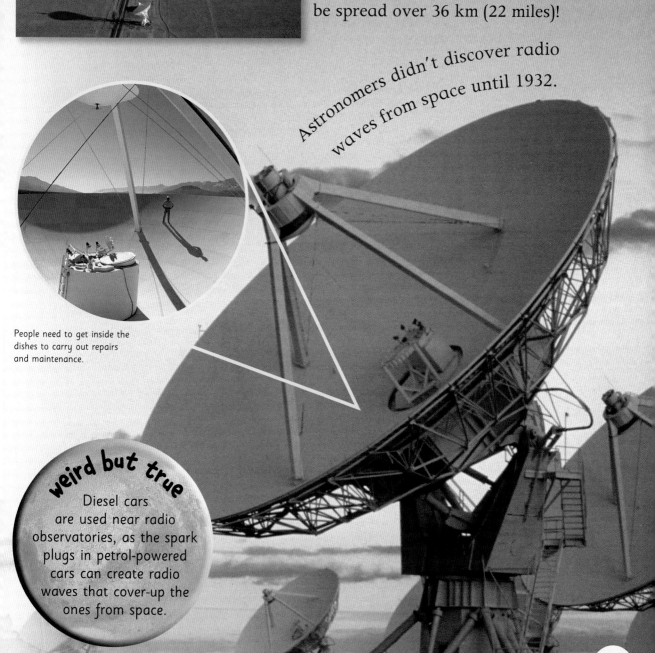

People need to get inside the dishes to carry out repairs and maintenance.

weird but true

Diesel cars are used near radio observatories, as the spark plugs in petrol-powered cars can create radio waves that cover-up the ones from space.

Our place in space

Earth seems huge to us – after all, it can take you a long time just to travel to school! But Earth is only a very tiny part of space. So where exactly does it belong in the Universe?

Earth looks like a swirly blue marble suspended in space.

The Earth and its moon

Earth, our home in space, has one natural satellite, our moon. The moon is about one quarter the size of Earth and, on average, it orbits about 384,000 km (240,000 miles) from us.

Uranus   Saturn   Jupiter
Venus   Mercury   Earth
Mars
Neptune

This picture shows where the planets are located. None of them, or their orbits, are drawn to scale.

Astronauts who have seen Earth from space are struck by its beauty. One described it as looking like a Christmas-tree decoration.

The solar system

Earth is the third planet from the Sun, at just the right distance from it to support life. The eight planets that orbit the Sun (plus moons, comets, asteroids, meteoroids, dwarf planets, dust, and gas) make up our solar system.

14

There used to be a ninth planet, Pluto, but this is now classed as a dwarf planet.

In a spin
Our galaxy has long curved arms that spiral out from a central bulge.

The Milky Way

Our Sun

The Local Group
The Milky Way is one of the largest galaxies in a cluster known as the Local Group. Millions of galaxy clusters make up the Universe.

The Milky Way
Our solar system is located in a galaxy called the Milky Way, a collection of billions of stars. It lies on the edge of one of the spiral arms.

Our home in space supports trillions of living things.

Great galaxies

A galaxy is a family of stars, gas, and dust held together by gravity. Much of a galaxy is empty space, with distances between each star that are hard to imagine.

Many galaxies are found in galaxy clusters, with thousands of members. Our galaxy, the Milky Way, belongs to a cluster of about 30 galaxies called the Local Group.

Two galaxies may sometimes collide. This image shows two spiral galaxies that have moved together.

A guide to galaxies

Galaxies differ enormously in size, shape, and mass, but they do fall into a basic pattern, depending on their shape (but we don't know what gives them a particular shape!).

Spiral galaxies
These disc-shaped galaxies spin slowly. They look a bit like whirlpools, and often have two arms that curl out from a central bulge.

Barred spiral galaxies
Barred spiral galaxies have arms that wind out from the ends of a central bar of stars rather than from the core.

Why are some galaxies named by letters and numbers?

Get mucky

Paint your own galaxy with white paint on black paper. Then splash drops of paint onto the paper to represent stars.

Collision course

Two galaxies may collide in a process that will take millions of years. The stars within the galaxy won't collide, but the gas and dust will – this collision can create new stars.

Irregular galaxies

These have no shape. They contain lots of gas and dust, and many are therefore active nurseries for the formation of new stars.

Elliptical galaxies

These are ball- or egg-shaped and largely made up of old stars. They don't contain the gas clouds for the formation of new stars.

Because there are so many. The names are codes that act like barcode numbers.

The Milky Way

Our solar system is a tiny – tiny! – part of a gigantic spiral galaxy, the Milky Way. This is made up of billions of stars, which look as if they have been sprinkled thickly onto the night sky.

Scientists think there are about 100,000 million stars in the Milky Way galaxy, but there may be even more.

Why is it milky?

Before the invention of telescopes, people could not see the stars very clearly – they were blurred together in a hazy white streak. The ancient Greeks called this streak a "river of milk". This is how our galaxy became known as the Milky Way.

Milky myths

Many myths have developed about the formation of the Milky Way.

Become an expert...

on stargazers, pages **8-9**

on our solar system, pages **50-51**

Native American stories tell of a dog dropping corn as he fled across the sky.

Kalahari bushmen say it was created by hot embers thrown up from a fire.

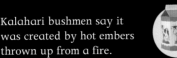

Hindu myth sees the milkiness as the speckled belly of a dolphin.

The ancient Egyptians believed the stars were a pool of cow's milk.

A side view
The Milky Way, like all spiral galaxies, is flat, with a bulge at the centre, and arms that circle outwards.

Where are the oldest stars in the Milky Way?

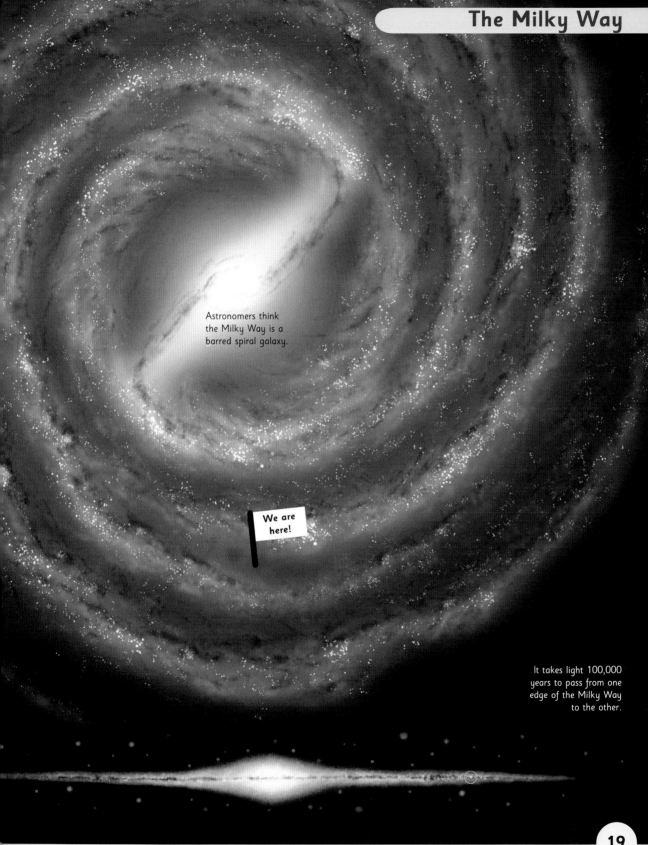

Astronomers think
the Milky Way is a
barred spiral galaxy.

We are
here!

It takes light 100,000
years to pass from one
edge of the Milky Way
to the other.

They lie towards its centre, often in giant balls called globular clusters.

Nearby stars

Our star is the Sun. It seems a very long way away, yet the Sun's light takes just over eight minutes to reach us. The light from our next-nearest star, Proxima Centauri, doesn't get to Earth for more than four years.

Sun

Light years away

Astronomers measure space distance in light years, because the distances are so great that normal measurements have little meaning. A light year is the distance light travels in a year.

Earth

How far is Proxima Centauri from Earth?

Why do stars twinkle?

Stars twinkle because of movements in the Earth's atmosphere. Starlight enters the atmosphere as straight rays, but air moves the light's path so it appears to flicker or "twinkle".

Proxima Centauri

Proxima Centauri was only discovered in 1915. It's very faint, so it can't be seen without the aid of a telescope. It looks red because it's a red dwarf star.

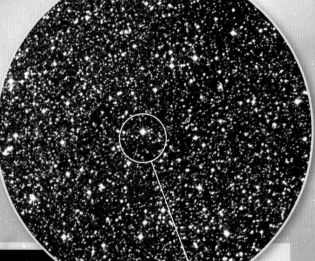

Proxima Centauri

We don't know whether Proxima Centauri has planets or not. This artist's impression shows what the view from one of its planets might look like.

Nearest neighbours?

Proxima Centauri lies in a group of three stars called Alpha Centauri. The others are Alpha Centauri A and Alpha B. Alpha A is like our Sun, so experts believe it may have planets that support life.

The Universe

The Universe takes in Earth and its moon, the Sun and the solar system, the Milky Way, the galaxies we know, and the galaxies we haven't yet discovered.

A typical galaxy contains over 100,000 million stars.

That's big...

The galaxies are spread over such unimaginable distances that even a space probe would take two billion years to cross our galaxy.

...and getting bigger

The Universe is still expanding, so all the galaxies are moving farther and farther apart.

How fast does *Voyager 1* travel?

Make your own Universe by drawing dots and spirals around a flat balloon to represent galaxies. As you blow air in, these "galaxies" move apart – that's what's happening to the Universe.

Dark mysteries

We can't see everything in space. Experts think there's lots of mysterious "dark matter" between the stars.

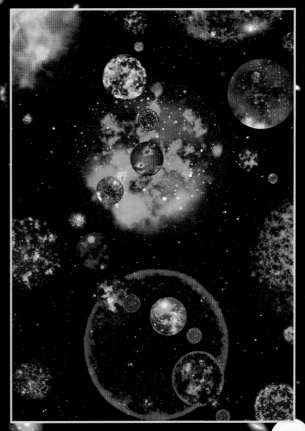

More of the same?
There might be other, parallel, Universes – experts call these the "multiverse".

Exploring space

When you're trying to imagine the vastness of space, consider that *Voyager 1*, more than 30 years after it was launched, is just reaching the outer edges of our solar system. Space exploration is just beginning.

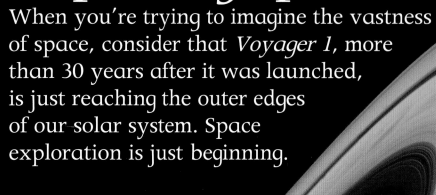

Saturn

Cassini orbiter

Astronaut
Leroy Chiao

Cosmonaut Yuri
Malenchenko

By any other name

The word astronaut comes from from two Greek words: *astron,* meaning star and *nautes,* meaning sailor. Russian astronauts are called cosmonauts (from the Greek words *kosmos*, meaning universe, and *nautes*, meaning sailor). Chinese astronauts are called *yuhangyuan* – literally "universe travel worker" or "space navigator".

How long did it take *Cassini-Huygens* to reach Saturn?

As the crow flies?

Spacecraft launched from Earth do not necessarily travel to their destination in a straight line. The *Cassini-Huygens* orbiter and probe, for example, took a roundabout route during its mission to Saturn in order to make use of gravity assists (see below).

The communications dish doubles as a sunshade to prevent overheating.

The main engines and rocket thruster clusters allow for steering and speed adjustments.

Curiosity quiz

Look through the Exploring space section and see if you can identify the pictures below.

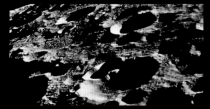

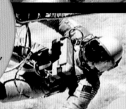

What is a gravity assist?
By flying past a planet and making use of its gravity to change speed and direction, a gravity assist helps spacecraft on their way. *Cassini-Huygens* travelled twice past Venus, once past Earth, and once past Jupiter before it headed for Saturn.

Become an expert...
about rockets,
pages 30-31

about space stations,
pages 38-39

Almost seven years

Astronaut in training

Astronauts do not just climb into a spacecraft and zip off into space – they need months of study and training first. They have to be in peak physical condition, and some astronauts claim their training is much harder than any mission.

Whatever it takes

Astronauts train for all sorts of situations. When necessary, they use real aircraft, equipment simulators, virtual reality systems, and computer simulations.

During an exercise, five NASA astronauts-in-training pull an "injured" crewmate to safety after a simulated parachute jump.

Underwater training

Floating in water is very like floating in space, so astronauts use special water tanks to train for space walks. One NASA tank can hold a full-size replica of the space-shuttle's payload bay.

How long is a NASA astronaut's training?

Around and around

A multi-axis trainer helps astronauts get used to the out-of-control spinning feeling they'll get from tumbling in weightless conditions.

Walking on the moon

At the NASA Lunar Landing Research Facility at Hampton, Virginia, USA, moon-walking practice involves suspending the astronaut by heavy cables.

Weightless wonder

Flown in a special way, an aeroplane with no seats and padded walls helps astronauts get used to feeling weightless. This plane is known as the "vomit comet" because its motion makes people feel sick.

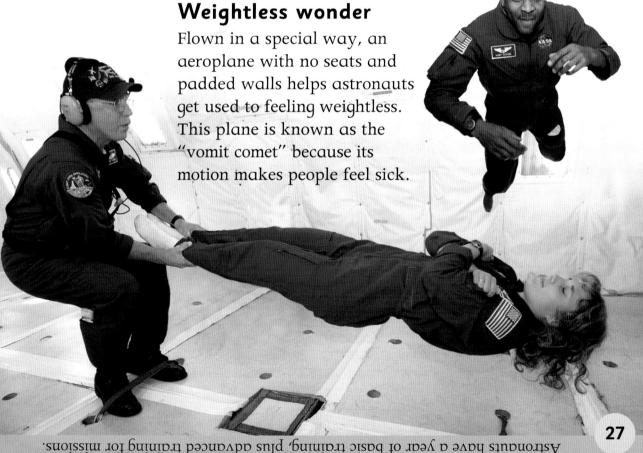

Astronauts have a year of basic training, plus advanced training for missions.

27

What's in your suitcase?

Just like you pack to go on holiday, astronauts pack lots of things to take into space. They wear different clothes depending on what they are doing.

Ready to go

During launch and re-entry, astronauts wear a special bright-orange suit, called a "pumpkin suit". Tools are stored in huge pockets on the legs.

Launch and Entry Suit

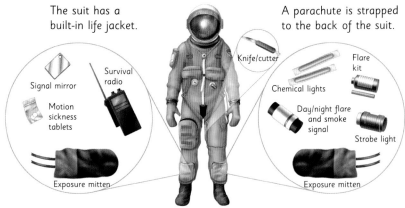

The suit has a built-in life jacket.

A parachute is strapped to the back of the suit.

Signal mirror

Survival radio

Motion sickness tablets

Knife/cutter

Chemical lights

Flare kit

Day/night flare and smoke signal

Strobe light

Exposure mitten

Exposure mitten

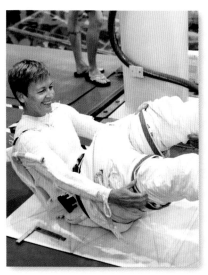

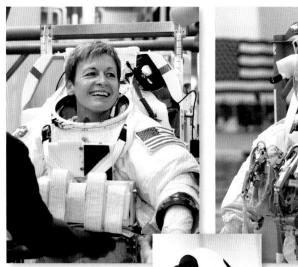

A peek underneath

For a spacewalk, astronauts need to wear an extravehicular mobility unit, or EMU. Underneath this, astronauts wear space underwear, a one-piece suit with small, water-carrying tubes that help keep them cool.

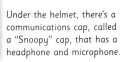

Under the helmet, there's a communications cap, called a "Snoopy" cap, that has a headphone and microphone.

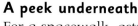

28

Can you guess how long an EMU can support an astronaut working in space?

A safe journey

Astronauts carry safety equipment in case of emergency.

 Life raft This is used if the crew have to crash land at sea.

 Sea dye This is used to colour water after an emergency landing to alert rescuers.

 Drink Astronauts must sip fluid regularly to prevent dehydration.

 Chemical light Astronauts carry lightsticks with them in the pocket of their suit.

Chill-out time

In space, astronauts wear clothes they would wear on earth, such as shorts and a T-shirt. Clothes are not changed as often as they would be on Earth – after all, there are no washing machines on board a space station!

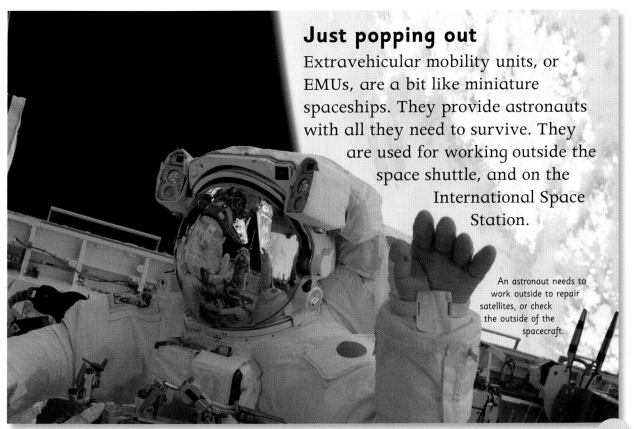

Just popping out

Extravehicular mobility units, or EMUs, are a bit like miniature spaceships. They provide astronauts with all they need to survive. They are used for working outside the space shuttle, and on the International Space Station.

An astronaut needs to work outside to repair satellites, or check the outside of the spacecraft.

Rockets

Rockets carry satellites and people into space. A rocket burns fuel to produce a jet of gas. The hot gas expands rapidly and is blasted downwards causing a force (the thrust) to push the rocket up.

A nose cone, or fairing, reduces air resistance as the rocket takes off.

Birth of the rocket

The first liquid-fuelled rocket was launched in 1926 by an American, Robert Goddard. It reached 12.5 m (41 ft). The flight lasted 2.5 seconds.

Launch of the *Long March 2C* rocket from the Jiuquan Space Centre, China on August 19, 1983. Its main cargo was a photographic imaging satellite.

Vostok 1 spaceship

On return, Yuri Gagarin parachuted from the *Vostok 1* capsule 7 km (just over 4 miles) above the ground.

First in space

The first person in space was the Russian cosmonaut, Yuri Gagarin. He was sent up in *Vostok 1* on April 12, 1961 for a 108-minute flight.

Long March 2C was 35.1 m (115 ft) long and 3.3 m (11 ft) wide.

How many tests were needed for the engine that powered the first stage of *Ariane 5*?

Types of rocket

There are many different kinds of rocket.

To escape Earth's gravity, a rocket has to reach just over 11 km (7 miles) per second. This is called the escape velocity.

 Reusable space shuttles carry people to and from the space station.

 Saturn V were the largest rockets ever built. They were used to launch all the moon landings.

 Firework rockets are used for celebrations.

 Military rockets have been used for hundreds of years.

 Experimental rockets provide information about fast and high flight.

 Some satellites have small rocket engines to position them once they are in orbit.

Ariane 5

Regular launches

Today, rockets such as *Ariane 5* are used to launch satellites into space. A satellite is a rocket's payload, or cargo, whose size determines whether it is sent up by a small or large rocket.

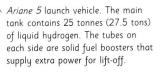

Ariane 5 launch vehicle. The main tank contains 25 tonnes (27.5 tons) of liquid hydrogen. The tubes on each side are solid fuel boosters that supply extra power for lift-off.

Biggest and best

The *Saturn V* were the largest, and most powerful, rockets ever built. They were used 13 times, between 1968 and 1972, including for the first moon landing.

Moon journey

During the 1960s there was a race between the USA and the former Soviet Union to put a man on the moon. The USA landed the first man on the moon with *Apollo 11* in 1969.

Apollo 11 reached the moon because of a huge rocket called Saturn V. Most of Saturn V contained the fuel needed to blast it into space. Three astronauts sat in a tiny capsule at the top of the rocket.

10 The service module is ejected before re-entry into Earth's atmosphere.

9

The journey back

11 The command module is the only part of the mission to return to Earth.

1 Five F1 engines blast the *Saturn V* rocket into space from the Kennedy Space Center.

12

Command module

Earth

The journey out

13

3 The command and service modules separate from the rocket and perform a 180° turn.

2 The rocket's engines fire to set the craft on a course to the moon.

The service module contained the power and life-support systems.

UNITED STATES

What was *Apollo 11*?
Apollo 11 was made up of three modules, or parts: the tiny command module, the service module, and the lunar module.

How many astronauts have walked on the moon?

Become an expert...

on the first moon landing, pages 34-35

on rockets, pages 30-31

6 The journey has taken 102 hours, 45 minutes. The lunar module is ready to land.

7 The command and service modules orbit the moon (one astronaut remains on board) while the lunar module lands. Two astronauts walk on the moon.

Moon

5 The rest of the rocket is discarded while the command, service, and lunar modules continue to the moon.

8 The lunar module joins the command and service modules so the two lunar astronauts can climb through. The lunar module is then abandoned.

The Eagle has landed

The lunar module (the part of *Apollo 11* that landed) was also known as the *Eagle*. It touched down on the surface of the moon on 20 July, 1969.

4 The command and service modules reattach to the lunar module, which is still connected to the rocket.

The three astronauts worked and slept in the command module.

Apollo 11

Mission commander Neil Armstrong struggled to find a flat landing site. He succeeded with just seconds to spare.

Men on the moon

On 20 July 1969, Neil Armstrong became the first person to walk on the surface of the moon. He was joined by Buzz Aldrin. A third astronaut, Mike Collins, remained in orbit with the command and service modules.

weird or what?

The lunar module computer on *Apollo 11* had just 71K of memory. Some calculators can now store more than 500K.

The lunar module was nicknamed the *Eagle*.

What did they do?

Armstrong and Aldrin spent almost 22 hours on the moon. About 2.5 hours of this was spent outside the *Eagle*, collecting rock and soil samples, setting up experiments, and taking pictures.

What was it like?

Buzz Aldrin described the moon's surface as like nothing on Earth. He said it consisted of a fine, talcum-powder-like dust, strewn with pebbles and rocks.

Why is there no blue sky on the moon?

Here comes Earth

Instead of the moon rising, the astronauts saw Earth rising over the moon's horizon – it looked four times bigger than the moon looks from Earth.

How did they talk?

There's no air in space, so sound has nothing to travel through. Lunar astronauts use radio equipment in their helmets.

Neil Armstrong

We have transport!

Three later *Apollo* missions each carried a small electric car, a lunar rover, which allowed the astronauts to explore away from the lander. These were left on the moon when the astronauts left.

This dish antennae allowed the astronauts to send pictures to Earth.

One lunar rover reached a top speed of 22 km/h (13.5 mph).

Splashdown

The astronauts returned to Earth in the *Apollo 11* command module. This fell through the atmosphere and landed in the Pacific Ocean. A ringed float helped to keep it stable.

Because the moon has no atmosphere.

Space shuttle

The first American space shuttle was launched in April 1981. This partly reusable craft has taught astronauts an immense amount about working in space.

Which bit is that?

The shuttle has three main components: the orbiter (the plane part, and the only part that goes into orbit), a huge fuel tank, and two rocket boosters.

Ditch the tanks!

The rocket boosters are released two minutes after launch. They parachute back to Earth and will be used again. The tank is discarded eight minutes after launch, and breaks up in the atmosphere.

Main (external) fuel tank

The orbiter carries between five and seven crew members.

Heat protection

Nearly 25,000 heat-resistant tiles cover the orbiter to protect it from high temperatures on re-entry.

Discovery

There are two rocket boosters, one on each side. Once lit, the boosters cannot be shut off; they burn until they run out of fuel.

The orbiter's engines are used once the orbiter reaches space.

weird but true

Woodpeckers delayed a space shuttle launch in 1995 by pecking holes in the fuel tank's insulating foam. Plastic owls are now used to frighten other birds away.

How long does it take the orbiter to reach space?

Pop it in there!
Each orbiter has a huge payload bay. You could park a school bus in this cavity, which holds the satellites, experiments, and laboratories that need to be taken into space.

The payload's doors open once the shuttle is in orbit.

The orbiter fleet

Five orbiters were built. Two have been lost in tragic accidents.

 Columbia first flew in 1981. It disintegrated on re-entry in 2003.

 Challenger was destroyed in 1986, just 73 seconds after launch.

 Discovery first flew in 1984. It marked the 100th shuttle mission in 2000.

 Atlantis first flew in 1985. It has completed more than 25 missions.

 Endeavour was built to replace *Challenger*. It first flew in 1992.

Space shuttle *Endeavour* landing at Edwards Air Force Base, California, USA.

A safe landing

Shuttles glide down, belly first. Once the orbiter touches the runway, it releases a 12 m (40 ft) drag chute to slow it down.

The future shuttle
NASA are currently working on designs for a new orbiter, the *Orion* Crew Exploration Vehicle (CEV). It will travel into space on an *Ares 1* rocket launcher, and carry up to six astronauts on each mission.

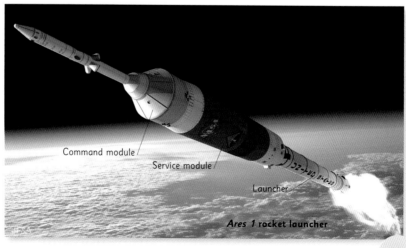

Command module

Service module

Launcher

Ares 1 rocket launcher

Space stations

Imagine living 380 km (235 miles) above everyone else, experiencing a sunrise or sunset every 45 minutes, sending your clothes to be burned up in the atmosphere rather than washed, and having no floor or ceiling. Welcome to life on a space station.

First ideas
Ideas for space stations existed a long time before they became a reality. In the 1950s, a 76 metre- (250 ft-) wide wheel-shaped design was proposed by space scientist Wernher von Braun.

Space stations
There have been ten space stations since 1971. They include:

 Salyut 1, launched in 1971 and in orbit for 175 days (of which 24 were occupied).

 Salyut 7, launched in 1982 and in orbit for 3,216 days (of which 816 were manned).

 Skylab, launched in May 1973 by the USA. It burned up in 1979.

 Mir, built in space by the Soviet Union, beginning in 1986. It fell into the atmosphere in March 2001.

A quick history
The first space station was launched in 1971. Since then a number of stations have orbited Earth. The International Space Station (ISS), has been built by 16 nations working together. The largest space station ever built, it's been occupied since 2000.

How many human beings have been sent into space?

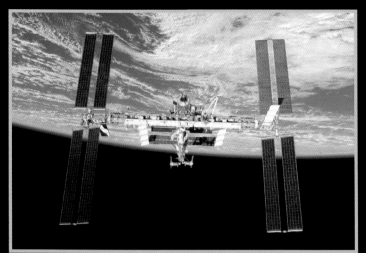

The ISS is constantly growing, as new parts are added.
This photograph was taken in 2007.

What is a space station?

It's a space laboratory that orbits Earth, operated by crews of astronauts who take turns living and working on it. Each crew stays for several weeks or months. Occasionally, an astronaut has stayed a whole year!

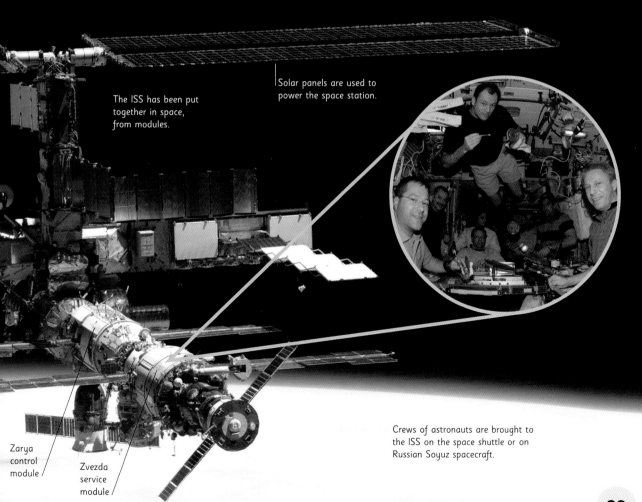

The ISS has been put together in space, from modules.

Solar panels are used to power the space station.

Crews of astronauts are brought to the ISS on the space shuttle or on Russian Soyuz spacecraft.

Zarya control module

Zvezda service module

Since 1961 more than 400 human beings have gone into space.

Living in space

A bed on the wall, baby wipes for a wash, footholds, and edible toothpaste! Life on a space station is very different from life on Earth.

Ordinary days

Astronauts need to do everything that you do. They eat, exercise, sleep, work, and play, but they have to do all these things in a home without gravity.

It's not easy to sort out bulky spacesuits in zero gravity!

New arrivals

When astronauts arrive at a space station, they bring supplies with them. Imagine trying to unpack your suitcase when you are floating!

weird but true

Some astronauts suffer temporary hearing problems after living on a space station. Why? Because the necessary air filters, fans, and pumps make it VERY NOISY!

Keeping fit

Astronauts' muscles don't work very hard in zero gravity so they quickly lose strength, so astronauts exercise for about two hours a day. This athlete completed a marathon on the International Space Station treadmill.

What is the longest period an astronaut has spent in space?

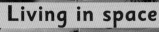

Time for work
Experienced scientists regularly join the astronauts in the space station to carry out a variety of experiments and record the results.

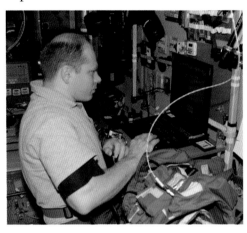

A tasty lunch?
Food is supplied in sealed packets and some of it is dehydrated. That means that water has to be added before the food can be eaten.

Time for bed
Most of the crew use sleeping bags, which have to be strapped to the walls of the space station. The bag holds astronauts' arms in place. Otherwise they would float above their head.

We like to keep clean, too!
Astronauts use combs and toothbrushes and toothpaste. But the toothpaste doesn't froth, and gets swallowed. Wet wipes are useful for a speedy wash.

Hair washing is possible, but rare!

Working in space

We have all seen workers on a construction site, hammering and drilling. Imagine a construction site floating in space high above the Earth's surface. That's what astronauts have to cope with when they are repairing a satellite, or putting together a space station.

The International Space Station (ISS) seen from the space shuttle *Discovery*.

Is it warm today?

In orbit, the strong sunshine heats astronauts up. Surprisingly, it's difficult to lose heat in space, so spacesuits have to include a refrigeration unit!

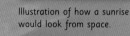
Illustration of how a sunrise would look from space.

An astronaut may be outside the space station for hours at a time. This one is working on the station's robotic arm.

Between 1998 and 2005, more than 60 spacewalks were performed. Each time two astronauts worked on the International Space Station.

Get mucky
Astronauts say that moving their hands in their gloves is difficult. To feel what they mean, put a rubber band around your closed fingers and try to open them. Do this fifteen times.

What does EVA stand for?

Large bowl-shaped antenna send and receive signals from satellites orbiting the Earth. These antenna can be turned to track a satellite as it moves across the sky.

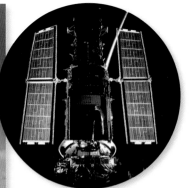

Charging up

Many satellites have huge solar panels that collect the Sun's rays. These make electricity to recharge on-board batteries that power the satellite.

What do they do?

Most artificial satellites are communication satellites, used for things like telephone calls, live television broadcasts, and computer link-ups. Other satellites help with a variety of different jobs, from guiding aeroplanes and ships to weather forecasting.

Weather satellites take pictures of Earth to show the type and location of clouds, and to measure land and sea temperatures. This is a hurricane moving across the ocean.

Satellite catalogue

There are many different types of satellite.

Communications satellites capture radio signals and send them to other places in the world. They help us to keep in touch.

Resource satellites take pictures of natural resources. These are sent to scientists, who turn them into maps of things such as oil deposits.

Navigation satellites are used by pilots and sailors to help them establish their position. In case of emergency, they can also pick up distress signals.

Military satellites are used by the armed forces for navigation, communication, and spying by taking pictures and intercepting radio waves.

Scientific satellites help experts to study the planets, the Sun, other solar systems, and things like asteroids, comets, and black holes.

Weather satellites help scientists to study weather. Like resource satellites, they have cameras, and they work in a similar way.

Sputnik 1, launched by the Soviet Union on 4 October 1957

Exploring Mars

Spacecraft have flown past Mars, orbited it, and landed on its surface. One day, we may even build a base on Mars. It may be cold, barren, and dusty, but it's full of possibilities.

Why study Mars?

At some point in its history, life may have existed on Mars. Although it's about half the size of Earth, it has clouds, weather patterns, and polar icecaps – once it even had active volcanoes. Learning about Mars may help us to understand our own planet.

On the barren surface of Mars, the robotic *Sojourner* rover examines a rock later nicknamed "Yogi".

Looking at Mars

There have been a number of missions to Mars.

In 1971, two spacecraft, *Mars 2* and *Mars 3*, got to Mars, but their landers failed to operate.

In 1976, two spacecraft, the *Viking* landers, tested for signs of life.

In 1996, *Mars Global Surveyor* was launched. It completed its first mission, but later lost contact.

In 1997, *Pathfinder* touched down, releasing a small rover called *Sojourner*.

In 1999, the *Mars Polar Lander* proved unsuccessful.

Seeing red

The landing craft that visited Mars took lots of pictures of its surface. These show a layer of soil that is rich in iron, which gives Mars its red colour – like rusty iron on Earth.

How much did it cost to build, launch, and land the Mars rovers?

What's happening now?

Two rovers, *Spirit* and *Opportunity*, have been exploring the Martian surface since 2004. They have sent back a wealth of data about the planet's surface, including plenty of evidence that there was once water on Mars.

The future on Mars

 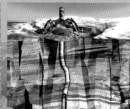

Scientists are always searching for ways to unlock the secrets of the red planet. Among the ideas suggested are an aeroplane that could travel across its surface (above left) and a thermal probe that would penetrate its ice caps (above right).

Cameras mounted on masts give scientists panoramic views of the Martian surface.

In order to explore the potential of a colony in space, eight scientists lived in a self-contained dome, *Biosphere II*, for two years during the early 1990s.

Nasa rover
Spirit

This image shows a 9 mm (.35 in) hole in Mars' surface drilled and photographed by *Spirit*.

The rover is powered by solar panels.

Living on Mars

If we do establish a base on Mars, it will have to be a self-contained structure that protects its inhabitants from both the atmosphere and the Sun's radiation. Below is an artist's impression of what a Martian base might look like.

Reach for the stars!

Long before the first spacecraft blasted off, people imagined travelling to other star systems in the hope of finding new planets. Travel between the stars is called interstellar travel, and one day it may happen. But the difficulties are huge.

The main problem

Our fastest space ships travel at significantly less than one thousandth of the speed of light. In terms of the vastness of space, that's incredibly slow. If we are to explore further, we need faster craft.

Space travel

A Russian physicist named Tsiolkovsky had an idea for a spacecraft long before people went into space.

1903 model of Tsiolkovsky's futuristic spacecraft

weird but true

Daedalus wouldn't be able to stop at Barnard's Star, as to slow down would need as much fuel as to accelerate. So it would just whizz by taking pictures and measurements.

Project *Daedalus* was planned as an unmanned space probe. It would travel at 12 per cent of the speed of light, reaching Barnard's Star within 50 years.

What's been done?

A long-term study into a possible interstellar spaceship took place in the 1970s. It was based on a mission to reach Barnard's Star, almost six light years away. The proposed spacecraft was named *Daedalus*.

If interstellar travel means travel between the stars, what is intergalactic travel?

Enterprise uses warp drive to achieve faster than light (FLT) interstellar travel.

We've already been!

There have been lots of interstellar spaceships in books and films. One of the most famous is the *Star Ship Enterprise*, from *Star Trek*.

Are there other ways?

Recently, scientists have looked at using laser powered solar sails for interstellar travel. The sail would have to be huge to collect enough energy to power the craft. It would move along because of the force of light bouncing off it. It would be helped along by powerful lasers aimed at the (mirrored) sail.

The reality

Our moon is about 1.25 light seconds away. Our fastest manned spacecraft take 3 days to reach it. The fastest spacecraft yet built, *Helios 2*, would take some 19,000 years to reach our nearest star, Proxima Centauri (4.23 light years away).

Earth is a long way from its neighbours in terms of possible space travel.

The solar system

The solar system is the name given to our immediate neighbourhood in space. It is made up of a star (the Sun), eight planets, more than 100 moons, and an assortment of comets, asteroids and other space rocks and dust. All of these are held captive by the Sun's gravity.

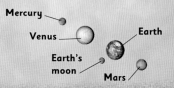

Mercury
Venus
Earth
Earth's moon
Mars

Inner planets

The asteroid belt (made up of millions of rocky bodies) circles the Sun. Mercury, Venus, Earth, and Mars are on the inner side of the belt.

Jupiter

Jupiter has sixteen moons. The largest four (Ganymede, Callisto, Io, and Europa) can be seen from Earth with binoculars.

What's in a name?

Most of the planets were named after Roman gods:
Mercury is the winged messenger (because it appears to move swiftly); **Venus** is named after the goddess of love (because it is the brightest and most beautiful planet); **Mars** is the god of war (because of its red, blood-like colour); **Jupiter** is named after the king of the gods (it is the largest planet); **Saturn** is the father of Jupiter and the god of agriculture; **Uranus** is the Greek god of the sky; and **Neptune** is the Roman god of the sea (named for its colour).

The planets circle, or orbit, the Sun, spinning as they move.

Outer planets

The planets outside of the asteroid belt are Jupiter, Saturn, Uranus, and Neptune. Pluto used to be the most distant planet, but it failed the new planet test (opposite).

Which planet is the smallest in our solar system?

What is a planet?

To qualify as a planet, an object has to meet a number of conditions:

 It must be in orbit around a star, just as Earth orbits the Sun.

 It must be large enough for its gravity to make it round.

 It must have cleared its orbit of other objects (which Pluto hasn't done).

It must not be a satellite (as, for example, the moon is a satellite of Earth).

Curiosity quiz

Look through the Solar System section and see if you can identify the pictures below.

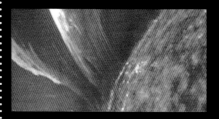

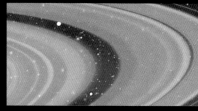

Saturn

 Every fifteen years, Saturn appears sideways to us and the rings seem to disappear.

Uranus

Neptune

Become an expert...

on the eclipse of the Sun, pages 54-55

on Venus, pages 58-59

The Sun

The Sun is white. Its colour is best seen when reflected in water. Never look directly at the Sun.

Our Sun is a star, but it is closer to us than any other star. Like all stars, it is a massive ball of burning gas, fed by constant explosions. Without it, our planet would be lifeless.

Shimmering lights can light up the skies towards the Earth's polar regions.

Long lived

The Sun was born just under five billion years ago. Although it burns four million tonnes (tons) of fuel each second, it is so big that it will continue to burn for another five billion years.

Solar wind

The Sun sends out a stream of invisible particles, called the solar wind. When these pass Earth's North and South Poles, they can create stunning colours.

Investigating the Sun

Various space probes have been designed to study the Sun.

Ulysses was launched in 1990 to look at the Sun's polar regions.

SOHO was launched in 1995 to observe the Sun and solar activity.

TRACE was launched in 1998 to study the Sun's atmosphere.

A hot spot?

White areas show places where the Sun's surface temperature is higher than elsewhere. Cooler, dark areas, called sunspots, sometimes appear on the surface.

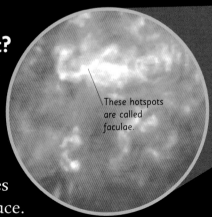

These hotspots are called faculae.

Does the Sun spin?

The size of
Earth compared
to the Sun.

The Sun is white, but
false colour images such
as this allow astronomers
to identify different
features on its surface.

It takes the Sun's heat about eight minutes to reach Earth.

Solar flares

Blasts of hot gas sometimes flare
up from the Sun's surface in
huge arcs or loops. They reach
thousands of kilometres (miles)
into space.

Yes, it does. It spins on its axis, like the planets of the solar system.

Eclipse of the Sun

It's a sunny day, but a shadow falls over the land. This is darker than a cloud covering the Sun: the light dims completely and for a few moments day turns to night. This is a solar eclipse.

The streaming light is the Sun's corona.

You are lucky if you see a total eclipse. You could wait hundreds of years to see two in the same place.

The Sun has been covered by the moon.

What is a solar eclipse?

Solar eclipses occur when the moon passes between the Sun and the Earth. By doing this, the moon stops some of the Sun's light from reaching Earth. The resulting shadow means that, temporarily, day turns to night in certain places.

People at the centre of the moon's shadow experience a total solar eclipse.

Earth

The moon

Sunlight

[Diagram not to scale]

How long would it take, if you could drive to the Sun?

The stages of a solar eclipse

Time-lapse photography shows how the moon covers the Sun in stages. In a total eclipse, the Sun will be completely covered – this is called totality – for up to eight minutes. The Sun's outer atmosphere, the corona, shows clearly at this time.

It takes about one hour for the moon to block the Sun's light, once its shadow begins to move across the Sun.

The moon's shadow sweeps across the Sun at about 1,700 km (1,100 miles) per hour.

The diamond-ring effect lasts for just a few seconds.

Ringed wonder

In the instant before the Sun disappears behind the moon, sunlight sometimes streams between mountains on the moon's surface, producing a stunning effect known as a diamond ring.

The map shows the paths of total solar eclipses to 2020.

Plotting eclipses

Solar eclipses occur once every 15 months or so and maps such as this one are used to plot the path of future eclipses. The shadow from a total eclipse follows a narrow path and often falls on an ocean – so it won't be seen (unless you're on a boat!).

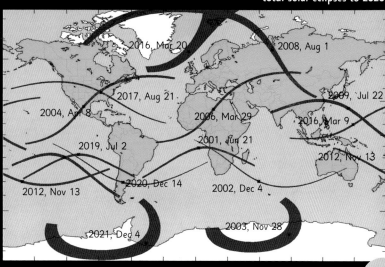

2016, Mar 20
2008, Aug 1
2017, Aug 21
2009, Jul 22
2004, Apr 8
2006, Mar 29
2016, Mar 9
2001, Jun 21
2019, Jul 2
2012, Nov 13
2012, Nov 13
2020, Dec 14
2002, Dec 4
2003, Nov 28
2021, Dec 4

About one hundred years. (And that's at top speed!)

Mercury

The closest planet to the Sun, and far smaller than Earth, Mercury has blistering hot days, but freezing nights. The nights get cold because Mercury has no atmosphere to trap the Sun's heat.

It takes 88 days for Mercury to orbit the Sun. So it has the shortest year of all the planets in the solar system.

Surface mapping
In 1974 and 1975, the space probe *Mariner 10* flew within 327 km (203 miles) of Mercury's surface. It took hundreds of photographs, covering just under half the planet.

An easy target
Mariner 10 provided close-ups of Mercury that showed a heavily scarred surface. Rather like our moon, this planet has been battered by comets and meteors. This is partly because there's no protective atmosphere in which meteors can burn up.

weird but true

One of Mercury's craters (the Caloris Basin) is so large that the British Isles could fit comfortably into it.

Many of Mercury's craters are named after famous painters, authors, and musicians. So you'd find Mozart, Beethoven, Michelangelo, and Bach there.

In Roman mythology, who was Mercury?

Red hot

As Mercury faces the Sun, temperatures reach a sizzling 425°C (800°F), hot enough to melt lead. Mercury is the second hottest planet, after Venus.

A patchwork picture of planet Mercury created using images taken by *Mariner 10*.

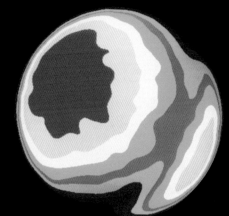

A temperature map of Mercury – red shows where the most heat is found.

A small planet

Mercury is the smallest planet in the solar system. Pluto, which is smaller, has now been reclassified as a dwarf planet.

Cross-section of Mercury showing its molten iron core.

Long journey

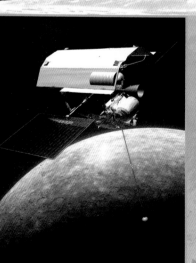

Launched in 2004, space probe *Messenger* set out on a journey to Mercury. Its aim: to reach the planet in 2008, fly by three times, then enter orbit around it in 2011. This close to the Sun, *Messenger's* heat shield will reach 370°C (700°F).

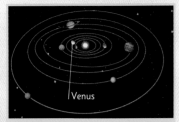

From Earth, Venus is easiest to see when it appears to be farthest in the sky from the Sun.

The morning star

You wouldn't want to visit Venus. You'd be crushed in an instant and your remains fried to a crisp. This barren planet is covered in acid clouds, and it has an incredibly dense atmosphere.

Where is it?

Venus is the brightest planet. It can be seen in the early-morning or early-evening sky, depending on where it is in its orbit around the Sun. That's why it's known as the morning or evening star.

A mass of clouds

The cloud layer is too thick to let much sunlight penetrate, but it does reflect a lot of light. In fact, after the moon, Venus is the brightest object in our night sky.

Venus's rocky plains without cloud cover.

Caused by chemicals in the atmosphere, the dark cloud tops (shown exaggerated on this image) blow around the planet.

Which planet is the nearest in size to Earth?

So what is it like?
This false colour picture of Venus was made from data collected by probes, including the *Magellan* probe, sent to Venus between 1989 and 1992. The blue areas represent huge plains of solid lava. The white, green, and brown areas are higher land, such as hills, mountains, volcanoes, and valleys.

Become an expert...
on the red planet pages 64-65
on the ringed planet, pages 70-71

Venus has very long days since it takes 243 times longer to rotate on its axis than Earth does.

Surface of Venus
This view of the surface of Venus exaggerates the height of Maat Mons, the highest volcano on Venus, to show its slopes in more detail. Maat Mons is named after Ma'at, the Egyptian goddess of truth and justice.

The surface temperature is about 482°C (900°F).

Venus spins in the opposite direction to Earth, meaning the Sun rises in the west and sets in the east.

Venus. Its diameter is just 650 km (400 miles) smaller than Earth's.

Third rock from the Sun

Our home planet, Earth, is the only one in the
solar system capable of supporting life as we
know it. It's the right temperature because
it's neither too close to the Sun, nor too
far from it.

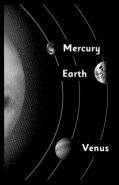

Mercury

Earth

Venus

Earth is the third planet from
the Sun. It takes Earth 365.25
days to orbit the Sun.

Take a deep breath

All planets have an
atmosphere made up of
gases – Earth's is mostly
nitrogen and oxygen,
with traces of carbon
dioxide and other
gases mixed in.

On this globe,
the ocean's warm
areas are coloured
red, and its cooler
areas are blue.

A warm blanket

Earth's atmosphere and oceans play
a crucial role in keeping its temperature
stable. They absorb the Sun's heat and
move it around the planet. This helps keep
the temperature suitable for life.

Which two planets lie between the Earth and the Sun?

Cut open an onion, and you'll see that it's composed of layers. Earth has layers too, and they get hotter and hotter the deeper they go.

A moving crust

Earth's surface layer, or crust, is a shell of solid rock. This crust is broken up into plates, which shift around constantly on a middle layer of molten, or liquid, rock. Earth's core is solid.

Earth's plates

Earth is constantly spinning. It takes 24 hours to turn completely on its axis.

Danger zones

The areas where Earth's plates move against each other are often weak spots where volcanoes and earthquakes are common.

Molten lava erupts from a volcano in Hawaii, which is located where there is a weak place in the Earth's crust.

Earth is surrounded by a thin halo — our precious atmosphere.

Earth is the only planet in our solar system with an atmosphere that animals and plants (as we know them) can breathe.

Become an expert...

on Earth's atmosphere, pages 6-7

Mercury and Venus...

The moon

Earth has one natural satellite: the moon.
It is the brightest object in the night sky
(though it doesn't produce its own light).
It is a bleak place, with no water, no
plants, no air, and no life.

Stretched flat, the moon's surface would just cover North and South America.

Spinning around and around

It takes 27 days for the Moon to travel around,
or orbit, Earth. As it travels, it spins. Slowly.
It actually spins just once during each orbit of
the Earth.

Moon's orbit

From Earth, we only see the nearside of the moon.

Earth

The farside of the moon is never seen from Earth.

Only one side of the moon is

The moon may have been formed after an immense collision that sent debris into orbit around Earth.

How did it form?

Nobody really knows, but
it was possibly after Earth
was hit by another planet
some 4.5 billion years ago.

Why does the moon produce so much light?

The Sun alters the tides, too.

The moon's gravitational pull gives Earth's oceans a bulge. Sea levels change in particular areas as Earth spins.

The red arrow represents Earth's rotational spin.

ever seen from the Earth.

The moon

Tide control

The twice-daily rise and fall of Earth's oceans is mainly caused by the moon's gravitational pull, which makes the ocean bulge a few metres in one direction. This bulge moves very slowly, but appears to sweep round the Earth as it turns.

Away from the bulge, it's low tide.

As a place passes through the bulge, it's high tide.

Moon missions

Many unmanned space probes have been sent to investigate the moon, including these below.

Luna 3, a Soviet probe, took the first pictures of the far side of the moon.

Lunar Prospector, a US probe, discovered ice near the Moon's poles in 1999.

Luna 9, a Soviet probe, made the first soft landing on the Moon in 1966.

A battered past

The moon has been badly battered by meteors in its long history, leaving its surface full of craters.

It doesn't produce any light. It reflects the Sun's light.

63

The red planet

Our nearest neighbour, Mars, was named by the Romans after their god of war, because its red colour reminded them of blood.

Mars is the fourth planet from the Sun. It has an atmosphere, seasons, huge mountains, and icy poles.

Earth

Mars

A Martian day lasts a little over 24 hours (24 Earth hours,

An alternate Earth?

Mars is half the size of Earth, and conditions are very different to those on our planet. Although Mars has a thin atmosphere and seasons, nothing grows there. Its red, desert-like surface is littered with dust and rocks.

I spy two moons

Mars has two lumpy moons that were discovered in 1877. They are so tiny that astronomers think they were asteroids pulled into orbit around Mars by its gravity.

Phobos

Deimos

Deimos (which means "terror" in Greek) is 16 km by 12 km (10 miles by 7 miles).

Phobos (which means "fear" in Greek) measures 28 km by 20 km (17 miles by 12 miles).

Is the Martian sky blue, like ours?

Is there water?

Surface temperatures on Mars are too low for liquid water to exist and Mars has no rivers, seas, or oceans. However, there was water once. We know this because of the existence of dried-up water channels.

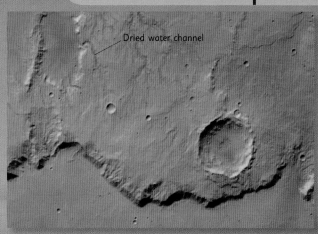

Dried water channel

39 minutes and some seconds). It is called a "sol".

A face on Mars

In 1976 *Viking Orbiter 1* sent a series of shots that showed a "face" on the planet's surface. Many saw this as an enormous sculpture built by intelligent life. It's actually a mountain.

Recent picture of the "face"

The first blurry picture of the "face".

That's definitely Martian!

There are a number of notable features on the surface of Mars.

The planet experiences strong winds that create immense dust storms.

Mars has a huge polar ice cap. If melted, the water would cover the planet.

The Olympus Mons volcano is the largest in the solar system.

The Valles Marineris canyon would stretch across the USA.

No. If you stood on Mars, you would see a pink sky.

King of the planets

Jupiter, the solar system's largest planet, is a gas giant made up mainly of hydrogen. It is huge. If all the planets in the solar system were combined, Jupiter would still weigh more than twice as much.

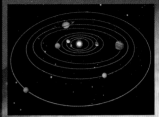

Jupiter is the fifth planet from the Sun. More than 1,300 Earth-sized planets could fit into Jupiter.

A thick cloud cover

Jupiter's cloudy atmosphere is about 1,000 km (600 miles) deep, but the clouds do not hide a solid crust. They swirl over an inner liquid layer of hydrogen and helium.

The Great Red Spot reaches about 8 km (5 miles) above the surrounding clouds.

Winds reach 400 kmh (250 mph) in the Great Red Spot.

Jupiter's bands are caused by the movements and mixing of different gases in the atmosphere as the planet spins.

A perfect storm

The Great Red Spot is a permanent hurricane that, in size, is twice the diameter of Earth. Observed since 1666, its swirling mass takes about a week to turn anti-clockwise.

Can you think why the *Galileo* spacecraft was so named?

As seen from space, Earth's colour scheme comes from its land, oceans, and white clouds. Jupiter is painted in oranges by the exotic chemicals in its atmosphere.

Jupiter takes 12 years to orbit the Sun.

In a spin

Despite its size, Jupiter spins faster than any other planet. In fact, one rotation takes just under 10 hours. It spins so fast that it bulges slightly at the equator, and its clouds are pulled into thick bands.

weird but true

Jupiter is shrinking slightly each year because it is being squeezed by its gravity. The energy produced means it produces more heat than it gets from the Sun.

Let's take a closer look

The *Galileo* spacecraft reached Jupiter in 1995 and began to orbit the planet. It also dropped a probe into Jupiter's atmosphere. Before being destroyed after just 58 minutes in the intense heat and pressure, the probe sent back information about the planet.

Galileo ended its long mission when it dropped into Jupiter and was destroyed in 2003.

This is Io, one of Jupiter's many moons, orbiting the planet.

The probe entered Jupiter's atmosphere at 170,000 km/h (106,000 mph). Its descent was slowed by a 2.5 m- (8 ft-) wide parachute.

The *Galileo* probe was about the size and weight of a fairly small cow.

No stopping me now!

The 5.3 m (17 ft tall) *Galileo* finished its main mission in 1997, but incredibly it survived until 2003, sending back lots of extra information about Jupiter and its moons. You can discover more about Jupiter's moons on pages 68 and 69.

It was named after Galileo Galilei, who used a telescope to observe Jupiter in 1610.

Jupiter's moons

Jupiter has 63 known moons (and probably many more that haven't yet been spotted). Most are tiny, and dark in colour. Scientists think many of them are asteroids that have been caught by Jupiter's immense gravity.

Ganymede, the solar system's largest moon, makes our moon seem rather small.

Europa

The Galilean moons

Jupiter's largest moons are named Io, Europa, Ganymede, and Callisto. One of its moons, Io, was shown by *Voyager 1* to have volcanoes that are so active that its surface is constantly being torn up.

There are rings, too

Jupiter also has a ring system, which was first seen in images captured by the *Voyager 1* space probe in 1979. The rings were formed by dust kicked up when meteorites have hit Jupiter's four inner moons.

Moon spotting

The four largest moons were named by a German astronomer, Simon Marius. They were studied by Galileo Galilei in 1610 (who thought at first that they were small stars). They can be seen from Earth with good binoculars.

Simon Marius

Io

Become an expert...

on Jupiter, pages 66-67

on our moon, pages 62-63

Who is credited with discovering Jupiter's largest moons?

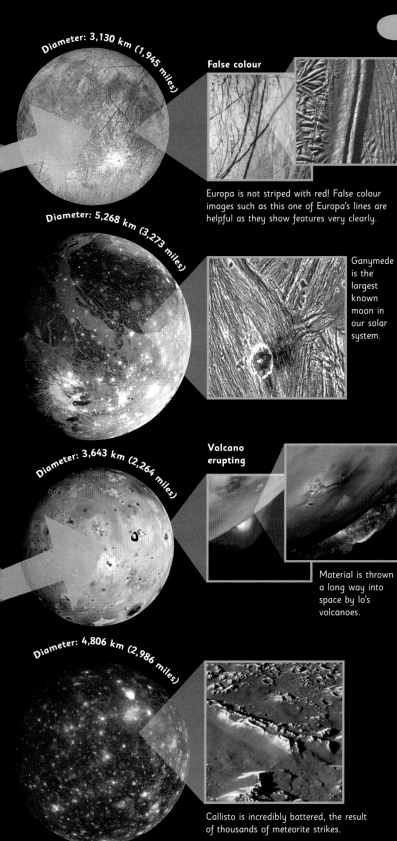

Diameter: 3,130 km (1,945 miles)

False colour

Europa is not striped with red! False colour images such as this one of Europa's lines are helpful as they show features very clearly.

Diameter: 5,268 km (3,273 miles)

Ganymede is the largest known moon in our solar system.

Diameter: 3,643 km (2,264 miles)

Volcano erupting

Material is thrown a long way into space by Io's volcanoes.

Diameter: 4,806 km (2,986 miles)

Callisto is incredibly battered, the result of thousands of meteorite strikes.

Europa has an icy surface criss-crossed with lines that suggest deeper activity. Scientists believe the ice may cover a liquid salty ocean, with a possibility of aquatic life. In fact, it has become the most likely place for extraterrestrial life in our solar system.

Ganymede is larger than Mercury, but it is not a planet as it doesn't orbit the Sun. Scientists think this moon has a molten core, surrounded by a rocky mantle, possible salt water, and an ice shell.

Io is constantly undergoing volcanic eruptions across its surface, the result giving it an amazing yellow-orange colour. In fact it has more than 100 active volcanoes! The eruptions happen because this moon is continually tugged and pushed around by the gravities of the other three.

Callisto's dark and dirty, icy crust is covered with craters. The largest, Valhalla, has shockwaves that spread out some 3,000 km (1,865 miles). Astronomers believe the crust hides a rocky core.

Galileo Galilei, though Simon Marius claimed to have spotted them in 1609.

Saturn

Saturn is the second largest planet in our solar system. It is huge. You could line up nine Earths in a row across Saturn, but as it is largely composed of gas, you couldn't land a craft on its surface.

Saturn is the sixth planet from the Sun in the solar system.

A ringed beauty

Saturn isn't the only planet with rings, but it is the only planet whose rings are visible to us because of their large area. The rings are made up of ice, dust, and rock.

Saturn spins around once every 10 hours 39 minutes, making it bulge at the middle as it spins.

Ice in Saturn's rings reflects light. That's why we see them so well.

Saturn is named after the Roman

Blown away

Even if you could land on Saturn, you'd be blown away pretty quickly by the incredibly strong winds. Winds around the planet's equator can reach 1,800 kilometres (1,100 miles) an hour.

High winds on Earth would be very light winds on Saturn.

Which other planets have rings, even though we can't see them?

Become an expert...

on *Cassini-Huygens*, page **25**
on planet names, pages **50**

The seven main rings are made up of about 10,000 ringlets. They extend more than 300,000 km (180,000 miles).

Saturn's rings are less than 1 km (.6 mile) thick.

A mission to Saturn

In 1997, the *Cassini* spacecraft blasted off for Saturn with a spaceprobe named *Huygens* on board. *Cassini* went into orbit around Saturn in June 2004 and *Huygens* was dropped onto its largest moon, Titan, in January 2005.

Vital statistics

Cassini sent back lots of information because of some amazing features:

The craft contains more than 12 km (7.5 miles) of wire.

It is the size of a coach, but is only a little heavier in weight than an elephant.

More than half its weight is made up by its fuel.

It carries a camera that could spot a coin from almost 4 km (2.5 miles).

Titan is difficult to study because of its thick orange clouds.

Huygens

Huygens is now the furthest human-made object ever to land on a celestial body.

I'm still here!

Huygens transmitted data for about five hours, but only about two hours was picked up before *Cassini* lost the signal after moving over Titan's horizon and therefore out of range. It remained active for far longer than anyone had hoped.

Distant twins

Uranus and Neptune are the
seventh and eighth planets
from the Sun, and are
often referred to as twins
because of their similar
size and make-up.

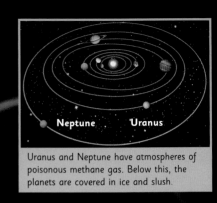

Uranus and Neptune have atmospheres of
poisonous methane gas. Below this, the
planets are covered in ice and slush.

Uranus

Uranus was discovered
in 1781 by William Herschel.
He named it *Georgium Sidus*,
or George's Star, in honour
of King George III of Great
Britain. This name was not
popular, so it was later
renamed Uranus.

Colours
Uranus looks a lot
plainer than this
false colour suggests,
but this image gives
astronomers a lot of
information about
the planet.

Uranus is encircled by
at least 11 narrow
rings made of rocks
and dust.

Unlike the other planets,
Uranus orbits the Sun
on its side.

This close-up picture
shows Uranus's rings.

Unusual seasons
It takes 84 years for Uranus to orbit the
Sun. The poles each experience 42 years
of "winter", then 42 years of "summer".
For 21 of those years, they are each in
continual darkness or light.

In Greek mythology, who was Uranus?

Neptune

A blue planet, Neptune is named after the ancient Roman god of the Sea. Neptune takes 165 years to orbit the Sun. So since its discovery in 1846, it hasn't completed a full orbit. It is due to do this in 2011.

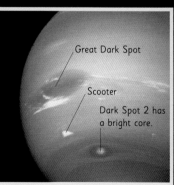

Distant twins

Neptune's moons
Neptune has 13 known moons. Its largest moon, Triton, is bitterly cold and has a heavily pitted surface as well as active volcano-like eruptions.

A day on Neptune lasts 16 hours 7 minutes.

 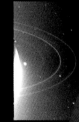

These two pictures show the rings of Neptune. The planet has at least four faint rings made up of dust particles.

Neptune is a very cold planet. This isn't surprising as it is 30 times further away from the Sun than the Earth. Imagine, from Neptune the Sun probably looks as small as the stars look to us.

Big storm
Neptune is incredibly stormy. In 1989 *Voyager 2* discovered a storm the size of Earth on Neptune's surface. The storm lasted several years.

Pictures from space
Voyager 2 has flown past both Uranus (in 1986) and Neptune (in 1989). It discovered ten of Uranus's moons and six of Neptune's. Most information had to be gathered in just a few hours as it sped on its way.

Miranda (one of Uranus's moons).

Titania (one of Uranus's moons).

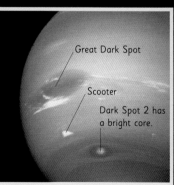

Great Dark Spot

Scooter

Dark Spot 2 has a bright core.

Neptune, taken by *Voyager 2* in 1989, showing two dark storms (the Dark Spots) and the fast-moving cloud Scooter.

Pluto

Pluto, a ball of ice and rock, was discovered in 1930, and became our solar system's ninth planet. However, in 2006 it was reclassified as a dwarf planet.

Why isn't it a planet?

Pluto was reclassified as it is just one of many objects in what is known as the Kuiper Belt. Other named dwarf planets in our solar system are Ceres and Eris.

The Kuiper Belt is a band of comet-like objects that orbit the Sun beyond Neptune.

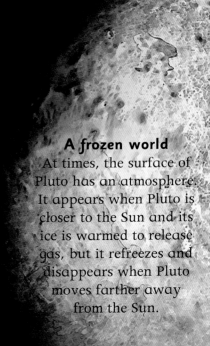

A frozen world
At times, the surface of Pluto has an atmosphere. It appears when Pluto is closer to the Sun and its ice is warmed to release gas, but it refreezes and disappears when Pluto moves farther away from the Sun.

So how big is Pluto?

Pluto is estimated to be about 2,300 km (1,400 miles) in diameter. Eris is some 3,000 km (1,864 miles) in diameter. Even some of the solar system's moons are larger than Pluto, including our moon!

Pluto	Moon	Earth
(2,300 km)	(3,400 km)	(12,750 km)
1,400 miles	2,100 miles	8,000 miles

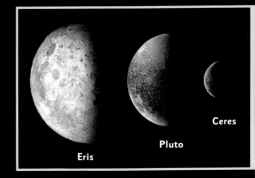

Eris

Pluto

Ceres

Can you guess how long it takes the Sun's light to reach Pluto?

Pluto's orbit

Pluto orbits the Sun slightly differently to the main planets. Its orbit also takes it nearer the Sun than Neptune for part of the 248 years of its orbit.

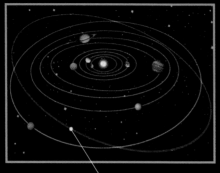

Pluto doesn't lie in the same plane as the eight planets of the solar system.

Pluto's surface is thought to be frozen nitrogen, which gives off gas if its temperature is raised.

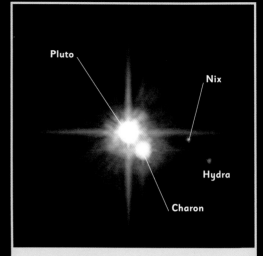

Pluto has three moons. The largest is called Charon. It moves around Pluto every six days. Two smaller moons, Nix and Hydra, were discovered in 2005.

New Horizons

Pluto takes 248 Earth years to orbit the Sun.

Scientists hope to learn a lot about Pluto when *New Horizons* reaches the dwarf planet.

New Horizons blasted into space on board an *Atlas 5* rocket.

Dwarf planets

Just look at this picture comparing the size of Pluto with other dwarf planets. Eris was only discovered in 2003. Ceres is the largest asteroid in the asteroid belt.

A mission to Pluto

In 2006, the US space agency NASA launched a spacecraft called *New Horizons* that is currently heading for Pluto. It will take ten years to make the 5 billion km (3 billion mile) journey.

It takes about 5 ½ hours.

Comets and meteors

In between the planets, space isn't empty. There is gas and dust, rocks called asteroids, and even comets – which can be thought of as space snowballs. Some comets are so small you probably wouldn't see them. Some are the size of islands.

Collision course

In 1994, a ball of fire the size of a small planet exploded on Jupiter. It happened when the first of more than 20 fragments of a comet ploughed into the planet.

Crash landing
When comet Shoemaker-Levy 9 collided with Jupiter, it was the biggest collision of two solar system bodies observed by humankind.

Comet Shoemaker-Levy 9 sent fireballs more than 3,000 km (1,900 miles) above the clouds of Jupiter.

How often are there meteor showers?

For six days, fragments of comet hit Jupiter.

Meteor shower

When pieces of comet burn up in the Earth's atmosphere, they produce meteor showers – bright shooting stars that race across the night sky, as in this picture of Leonid meteors.

Curiosity quiz

Look through the Comets and meteors section and see if you can identify the pictures below.

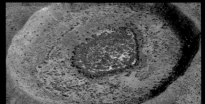

Spot the difference

Here's a guide to space objects you'll find in this section.

 Meteors, or "shooting stars", are particles of space dust that burn up as they enter Earth's atmosphere.

 Asteroids are basically giant boulders of rock, some so big that they have their own tiny moons.

 Meteorites are bits of space debris that survive hitting the Earth.

 Comets are space snowballs, made from dust and ice, that orbit the Sun.

 Space junk is man-made things that have been left or lost in space.

Become an expert...

on asteroids, pages 82-83

on space debris, pages 86-87

Just passing

Comets are huge, dirty space snowballs. Made of ice, rock, and dust, they hurtle through space on huge orbits around the Sun to the outer edge of our solar system.

Comets can reach tens of kilometres (miles) across.

A comet from Earth

In early 2007, the brightest comet for 40 years, comet McNaught, hit the skies. It was so bright that it could be seen night and day.

Distant visitor

The closest comet Hyakutake came to Earth was 15 million km (9.3 million miles). It was spotted in 1996 by a man in Japan who was looking through binoculars.

A comet's tail

Halley's comet

Comets often reappear at regular intervals as they travel past Earth. One of the most famous, Halley's comet, returns every 75 or 76 years. It is named after astronomer Edmund Halley who predicted it would return in 1758.

Edmund Halley
1656-1742

Halley's comet travels up to 240,000 km/h (150,000 mph).

What does the word "comet" mean?

can trail for millions of kilometres (miles).

Tail light
If a comet's orbit takes it close to the Sun, its surface begins to evaporate, releasing gas and dust. This results in a spectacular tail pointing away from the Sun.

Tail piece
A comet's tail has two parts – the yellow or white part is made up of dust. The blue streaks are made of gas. Sometimes it shows up as two tails.

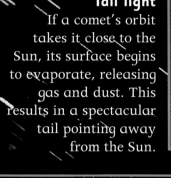

Tall tail
These pictures show how the comet's tail changes as it moves towards and then away from the Sun.

Halley's comet in 1910

Shooting stars

A flash of light briefly streaks across the sky, and then disappears. It is probably a meteor – a common sight. Meteors are also known as shooting stars.

Fragments of Canon Diablo meteorite from meteor crater in Arizona.

What is it?

A meteor is a chunk of rock or dust that burns up as it enters Earth's atmosphere. This happens about 90 km (56 miles) above the planet's surface. If a meteor smashes into Earth, it is called a meteorite.

Sparkling showers

When several fragments of a former comet or asteroid hit Earth's atmosphere and burn up, it can result in spectacular showers. One famous shower takes place every November, when Earth passes through a swarm of meteoroids called the Leonids.

Bomb blast

When the Wolf Creek meteorite crater was formed 1-2 million years ago it exploded like an atomic bomb. Nearly a perfect circle, the crater is 853 m (2,798 ft) in diameter.

Wolf Creek crater
Great Sandy Desert, Western Australia

How many meteors (most very small) hit Earth's surface each year?

Powerful meteorites

There have been a number of spectacular meteorite strikes on our planet.

Tunguska, Siberia
A meteorite strike destroyed miles of forest in 1908.

The meteor crater in Arizona was formed 50,000 years ago. It is 1,265 m (4,150 ft) across.

Dinosaurs
Many believe the dinosaurs were wiped out by a meteorite strike 65 million years ago.

Fire from the sky
People have feared meteorites for centuries. Some saw them as fiery dragons, others as weapons sent by angry gods.

A meteorite strikes our atmosphere at around 32 km (20 miles) per second.

Get mucky
See the impact of meteorites by dropping different size balls onto a tray of damp sand. This shows what happens when a meteorite hits a planet's surface; it leaves a crater.

I like you!
Most meteorites will attract a magnet, because of their iron content.

A lone meteor
A meteor that isn't part of a shower is called a sporadic meteor. Incredibly bright meteors are called fireballs.

We can't be sure, but it's probably about 1,000.

The asteroid belt

Asteroids are chunks of rock – some are small enough to hold in your hand, while others are larger than a mountain. Most of those in our solar system orbit the Sun within the asteroid belt, which lies between Jupiter and Mars.

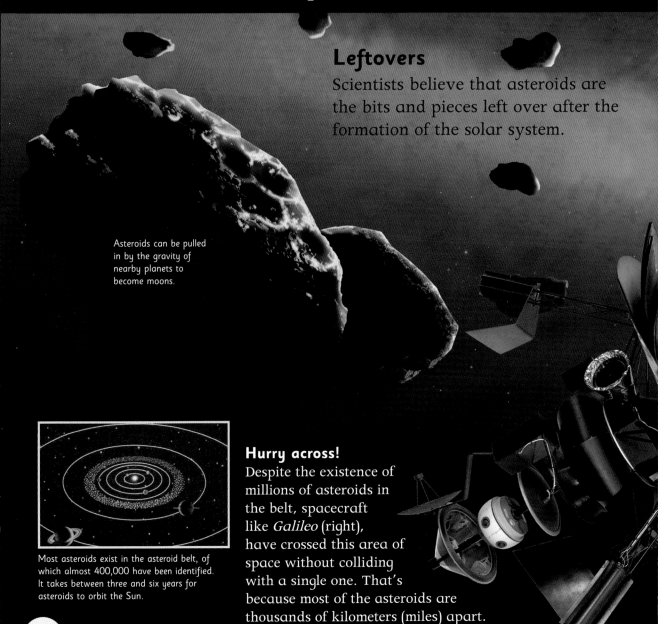

Leftovers

Scientists believe that asteroids are the bits and pieces left over after the formation of the solar system.

Asteroids can be pulled in by the gravity of nearby planets to become moons.

Most asteroids exist in the asteroid belt, of which almost 400,000 have been identified. It takes between three and six years for asteroids to orbit the Sun.

Hurry across!

Despite the existence of millions of asteroids in the belt, spacecraft like *Galileo* (right), have crossed this area of space without colliding with a single one. That's because most of the asteroids are thousands of kilometers (miles) apart.

Why aren't most asteroids spherical, like the planets?

A real whopper

The largest asteroid ever found in the belt was Ceres. It is the size of Texas, a state in the USA (about 933 km/580 miles wide). Modern experts classify Ceres as a dwarf planet.

Chicxulub crater in Mexico

Size is everything

The asteroid belt contains millions of asteroids. Scientists estimate there are more than 750,000 with a diameter larger than 1 km (0.6 mile), and 200 larger than 100 km (60 miles).

Collision course

Stray asteroids or comets occasionally collide with planets, creating huge craters. An asteroid may have crashed into Earth 65 million years ago, causing a catastrophic climate change that wiped out the dinosaurs.

Gaspra

Deimos

Phobos

Dactyl

Ida

Asteroids range in size and shape. Only the largest tend to be round.

Just passing

The *Galileo* spacecraft took the first clear photographs of an asteroid, when it passed through the belt enroute to Jupiter and shot Gaspra in 1991. It later took a picture of Ida (55km/35 miles long) when it passed through the asteroid belt again in 1993. The shot included its moon, Dactyl – the first evidence that asteroids can have satellites of their own.

Because they are too small. They lack the gravity to pull themselves into a ball shape.

Asteroid landing

Near Earth Asteroids (NEA) are asteroids that pass relatively close to Earth. This means they are the easiest asteroids for scientists to study, and in fact two spacecraft have successfully landed on NEAs.

The launch of NEAR spacecraft in 1996.

Asteroid Eros

Eros is about 33 km (20 miles) in length. The spaceprobe NEAR-*Shoemaker's* mission was to orbit Eros. NEAR stands for Near Earth Asteroid Rendezvous.

Asteroid Itokawa

One asteroid that has been studied is Itokawa. It is tiny. A Japanese spacecraft, *Hayabusa*, was sent to collect dust samples from Itokawa, and is now on its way back to Earth.

Hayabusa (which means "falcon" in Japanese) took this picture of Itokawa.

Itokawa was named after a Japanese rocket scientist.

Touchdown

Hayabusa landed on Itokawa on November 20th 2005, and remained on the surface for just 30 minutes. It landed again briefly on the 25th. Nobody's sure whether or not it picked up surface samples.

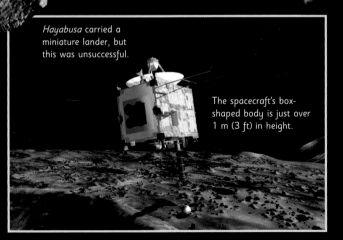

Hayabusa carried a miniature lander, but this was unsuccessful.

The spacecraft's box-shaped body is just over 1 m (3 ft) in height.

Eros is named after a Greek god. Can you guess which one?

Touchdown

At the end of its mission, in February 2001, the mission team decided to try landing the probe on Eros to show that it could be done. As it neared the asteroid for landing it sent a series of 69 increasingly detailed shots of the surface.

February 2000
Eros picture made up from six images pieced together.

January 2001
Taken from 38 km (24 miles) above Eros, showing a crater.

February 2001
Eros' surface taken from a distance of 700 m (2,300 ft).

What did the probe find?

Some asteroids are basically loose piles of rubble, floating together in space. Scientists discovered Eros to be solid. It is also very old – perhaps as old as Earth.

A close approach

NEAR-Shoemaker spent a year orbiting Eros, during which time it sent back lots of useful information to Earth about the asteroid.

It takes Eros just over five hours to rotate on its axis.

Researchers have said that a person who could jump 1 m (3 ft) on Earth, would be able to jump 1.6 km (1 mile) on Eros because of its weak gravity.

Eros was the Greek god of love.

Space debris

An astronaut works on a shuttle, and loses a tool. An ageing satellite begins to break up. A panel is knocked off a space station… space is littered with junk, and the problem is getting worse.

Cosmic litter

Examples of unexpected space rubbish include:

A glove, lost by an American astronaut on a space walk in 1965.

Rubbish bags, released by the Mir space station.

Two cameras, reported lost in space by astronauts.

Nuts and bolts, lost when satellites were being repaired.

Tracking the junk

An incredible amount of junk is orbiting Earth. The path of anything larger than a tennis ball is tracked by scientists – currently about 13,000 objects are being watched. Experts believe that, in total, well over 150,000 objects larger than 1 cm (0.5 in) are orbiting our planet.

At what height does space litter orbit the Earth?

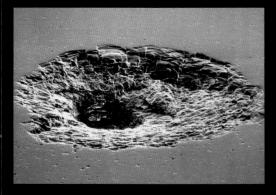

What are the dangers?

Items of junk are generally far apart in space, but problems arise when a fast-moving object (up to 28,200 km/h/17,500 mph) slams into a spacecraft or space station. This crater in a window surface on space shuttle *Challenger* is typical of the damage caused.

Mission controllers keep a close watch on the path of their space launches.

Falling to Earth

Debris falls to Earth regularly, but there is only one report of someone being struck by metal from space. After all, most of Earth is ocean.

Bits of space debris eventually fall into Earth's atmosphere, where they either burn up, or crash to the ground.

What can be done?

Before every launch, mission controllers make sure their spacecraft will not travel near any dangerous junk. Scientists are hoping to find a way to clear Earth's orbit, but a solution is a long way off. Suggestions being considered are: lasers that can break objects up; space-rubbish ships; and technology that can tug rubbish lower so it burns up in the atmosphere.

87

Most objects orbit between 700-2000 km (435–1,240 miles) above the ground.

Mysteries of space

Black holes, alien life, the Big Bang... space and its mysteries have always fascinated people, and inspired artists and writers. We know quite a lot about space, but there is far more we don't know. So what is fact, and what is fantasy?

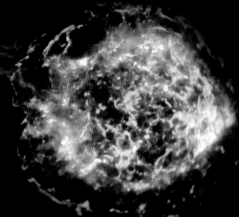

Lives of the stars

Other mysteries, such as how stars are born in nebulae and die in supernovae are gradually being solved with the help of incredibly powerful telescopes. But there is a long way to go.

Supernova remnant Cassiopeia A

Which novel about an alien invasion from Mars was published in 1898?

Illustration from 1950s sci-fi comic

Fact or fiction?
Curiosity about aliens has produced lots of ideas about what they might look like. In some books and films, aliens look much like humans with two arms and legs, while in others, they resemble giant blobs or spiders.

Curiosity quiz
Look through the Mysteries of Space pages and try to identify the pictures below.

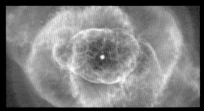

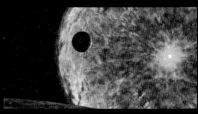

Storm trooper from Star Wars

Space monster toy

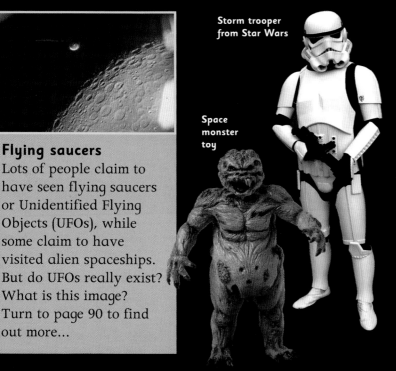

Flying saucers
Lots of people claim to have seen flying saucers or Unidentified Flying Objects (UFOs), while some claim to have visited alien spaceships. But do UFOs really exist? What is this image? Turn to page 90 to find out more...

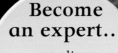

Become an expert...
on aliens, pages 92-93
on life on Mars, pages 94-95

UFOs

Flying saucer-shaped objects, crop circles, lights in the night sky... people have long claimed to see and find evidence of UFOs (Unidentified Flying Objects). Look at some of the claims yourself. What do you think?

Crop circles

These are intricate designs made from flattened areas of corn. Some believe they are the landing sites of flying saucers, but many have been proved to have been manmade.

Was it a strange craft?

The Apollo picture shown on the previous page was thoroughly investigated, and found to be nothing more mysterious than the floodlight boom, used when astronauts left the spacecraft.

A UFO comes in to land?...

The idea that intelligent life exists outside our solar system has always seemed to intrigue people. This cave painting is thousands of years old. It appears to depict an extraterrestrial encounter.

Which country do you think has the most reported incidents of UFOs?

weird but true

In the Bible, Ezekiel seems to describe the appearance of a UFO – at least, some people think so. He told of a fiery, wheeled object in the sky that shot lightning bolts.

Artists have often drawn space ships as metal oval discs.

In the news

Some newspapers have even reported the landing of alien spacecraft. The most famous of these incidents occurred at a place called Roswell, USA, when strange debris was found in 1947.

Waiting for an answer

This famous image, below, has still not been explained, though some suggest it may be the mirror from a truck. It was taken by a farmer in Oregon in 1950.

Is this a truck's wing mirror, or something more mysterious?

What was Roswell?

People claimed the debris found at Roswell was of a spacecraft that crashed. Early newspaper reports called it a "flying disc". However, the military said it was a top secret weather balloon.

Crash debris is investigated at Roswell in the 1940s.

Road sign in Roswell, USA, the scene of space ship investigations in the 1940s.

An alien spacecraft?

Roswell resulted in a number of books, films, stories, and general speculation. However, most people now believe that it was a weather balloon.

An Air Force Weather Balloon in 1955, eight years after Roswell.

Is anyone there?

If there are aliens, it is unlikely they will speak the languages of Earth, so communication may be a problem. Coded signals have been sent into space. People are also listening for signals from space.

SETI

The search for Extra Terrestrial Intelligence (SETI) uses powerful radio telescopes to scan for alien signals. However, so far nothing has been found.

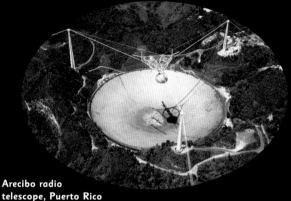

Arecibo radio telescope, Puerto Rico

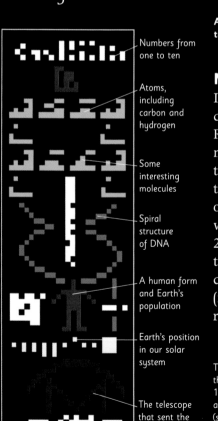

Numbers from one to ten

Atoms, including carbon and hydrogen

Some interesting molecules

Spiral structure of DNA

A human form and Earth's population

Earth's position in our solar system

The telescope that sent the message

Message into space

In 1974, astronomers at Arecibo, Puerto Rico, sent a radio message from us to the stars. It was sent towards a cluster of stars called M13, where it will arrive in 25,000 years. We may then get a reply after another 25,000 years (if anybody is there to read it!).

The Arecibo message lasts three minutes. It consists of 1,679 pulses, which when arranged form a pictogram (see left). The pictogram explains the basis of life.

This radio telescope is often used by the SETI institute.

The Parkes radio telescope, Canberra, Australia

Can you guess how many languages are spoken on Earth?

A plaque into space

The spaceprobes *Pioneer 10* and *11* carry engraved metal plaques. It is a space equivalent of a message in a bottle! The plaques reveal Earth's place in the solar system, the probes' route away from Earth, and give the outlines of a man and woman.

Pioneer spaceprobe

Gold-plated record with "Sounds of Earth" and cover for *Voyager 1*.

The record was mounted on a bracket on *Voyager 1*.

A record into space

The *Voyager* spacecraft, sent up in 1979 and 1981, each carried a gold-plated LP record, a disc that has encoded sounds and photographs that will provide an alien intelligence with an idea of life on Earth. There are greetings in 56 languages - and that includes a recording of whale song.

Become an expert...

on radio telescopes, pages 12-13
on other Earths, pages 100-101

93

Almost 7,000. Just imagine how many may be spoken in the Universe!

Is there life on Mars?

Historically, many people have believed that a race of creatures live on Mars. Representations have appeared in books, artwork, comics, on the radio, and on television and in films in many different forms. Do any of these creatures actually exist? No!

Two hundred years ago

In the 1780s, William Herschel observed seasonal changes around the Martian poles and noted that its inhabitants "probably enjoy a situation in many respects similar to our own".

William Herschel

Herschel's 12 m (40 ft) telescope

In the papers

In the 1920s, a newspaper report on the Martians claimed they would have "very large noses and ears and immense lung development... Their legs are poorly developed, because matter on Mars weighs less than here".

Guess how many canals on Mars Percival Lowell mapped?

One hundred years ago

The idea of intelligent Martian life reached a peak at the turn of the twentieth century, when a wealthy businessman, Percival Lowell (1855-1916) set up his own observatory in Arizona, USA, and began to study Mars.

Lowell claimed he could see a network of lines criss-crossing the surface of Mars, which he believed were built to transport water from the poles around the planet.

Martians sell books

We now know the lines weren't there, but many people believed Lowell's theories, caught up by the excitement of the idea. The discussions inspired H.G.Wells' *The War of the Worlds*, a book published in 1898.

Illustration from H.G.Wells' book *The War of the Worlds*.

In 1938, a radio dramatization of H.G.Wells' book by Orson Welles sent a million Americans into panic. The broadcast described the Martian invasion of Earth in the form of a news report.

A big prize!

In 1901, the French *Guzman* prize offered an award of 100,000 francs for the first person to make contact with extraterrestrials. Terms actually excluded contact with Martians as it was believed to be too easy!

Camille Flammarion's (founder of the Societe Astronomique) 'Flat Earth' woodcut influenced Pierre Guzman who offered the prize.

The Big Bang

Most scientists now believe that the Universe was born from a hot, dense spot more than 13 billion years ago. They call this event the Big Bang.

A Universe is born

What was later termed the Big Bang was first proposed by Georges Lemaitre in 1931. Scientists believe it was the beginning of everything, but don't know what caused it to happen.

Georges Lemaitre

As the Universe expands and cools, at 300,000 years, matter as we know it starts to form. The Universe is a thousandth of its size today.

What happened?

Space and time were brought to life from a minute speck, which was unbelievably hot and heavy. The energy contained in this speck immediately began to spread out, in the form of an ever expanding fireball.

The Big Bang: "a day without yesterday."

96

Do you think the Big Bang was an explosion?

A long time coming

Matter only began to form hundreds of thousands of years after the Big Bang – long after the fireball had cooled. The resulting gases would form the stars, planets, and galaxies that exist today.

At 9 billion years the Universe looks much as it does today, if a little bit smaller. Our Sun starts to form.

Stars and galaxies start to form after about 300 million years.

What's that?

Scientists have detected a faint radio signal, present in any direction they look for it in space. They believe it is a faint glow from the Big Bang's superhot fireball. It is called The Cosmic Background Radiation.

The Cosmic Background Radiation was discovered by American physicists Arno Penzias and Robert Wilson in the 1960s.

No beginning, no end

An alternative to the Big Bang, the Steady State Theory claimed there was no beginning or end for the Universe. It's just always been there. Few scientists now believe in the Steady State Theory.

weird but true

The astronomer who gave the Big Bang theory its name didn't support it. He termed it Big Bang as a criticism and was surprised that the name stuck. He believed in the Steady State Theory.

Black holes

Black holes are a great mystery. Astronomers know they are there, because of their effect on nearby stars (if a star is too close, it gets pulled towards the hole), but they have proved very difficult to study. Why? Because they are black, and that makes them invisible!

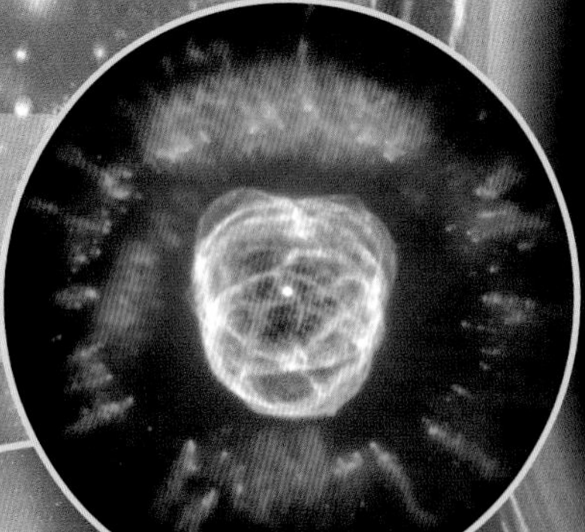

Scientists believe a black hole may be formed by the death of a star. This picture shows a star's explosion as it dies.

Sometimes some of the falling gas is squirted back out as hot jets.

This artist's idea of a black hole, shows clouds of gas and dust swirling rapidly around it before being pulled in towards the hole at the centre.

Why are they there?

Birth of a hole

Black holes are sometimes born when a star explodes and dies. When a big star has run out of fuel it can't stop gravity pulling its gas together, squeezing it tighter and tighter until it forms a tiny neutron star, or a black hole.

Into the hole

Black holes have such strong gravity that nothing in the surrounding space can escape, not even light. However, they do not act as enormous vacuum cleaners – something has to get close enough to be in danger of being pulled in. They are a bit like space whirlpools, affecting just their area of space.

How big can a black hole get?

This x-ray picture shows a black hole (the blue dot) at the centre of a galaxy with a mass 30 million times that of our Sun. The orange dots are just black holes eating stars that got too close.

How do we find the holes?

Scientists can find black holes because gas and dust falling into a hole rubs together and becomes incredibly hot. This gives off x-rays which space telescopes detect.

Later, the black hole's gravity would pull harder on the astronaut's feet than at their head.

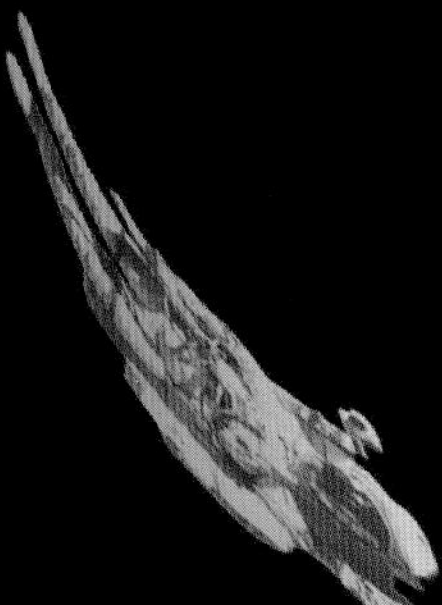

If an astronaut entered a black hole, at first he or she wouldn't notice.

The astronaut would be stretched into a long, thin, spaghetti-like shape, finally being crushed to an invisible speck.

What do they do?

Is that true?

Some people think a black hole may be a doorway to another universe. But it's all just speculation. Nobody really knows. However, it is doubtful someone could survive the journey through the hole to find out. An astronaut unfortunate enough to try would be stretched out like a piece of spaghetti.

They grow as they "eat", so they are only limited in size by the matter they consume.

99

Are there other Earths?

Astronomers know that there are planets outside our solar system. One day they hope to discover a planet that is capable of supporting life. The search has begun.

A recent discovery

Twenty light years away from us lies a star called Gliese 581. Astronomers have identified three planets orbiting Gliese. One is too hot for life, one is too cold, but one is in the Goldilocks zone – and it may be just right.

Gliese 581 is a red dwarf

Gliese 581c may be rocky – or it may be composed of gas. Nobody is really sure.

Gliese 581b takes 5.4 days to orbit its sun and is too hot to support life.

Gliese 581c takes 13 days to orbit its sun, and may be the right distance from it to support life.

How right?

Gliese 581c is thought to orbit in the Goldilocks, or "habitable zone", where the surface temperatures would allow liquid water.

How many planets do we actually know have life on them?

Compared to Earth

The planets we find are so distant that it is difficult to be sure of their size, or their composition.

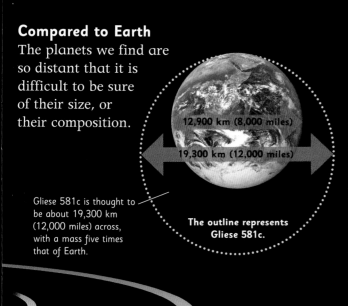

12,900 km (8,000 miles)

19,300 km (12,000 miles)

The outline represents Gliese 581c.

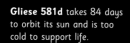

Gliese 581c is thought to be about 19,300 km (12,000 miles) across, with a mass five times that of Earth.

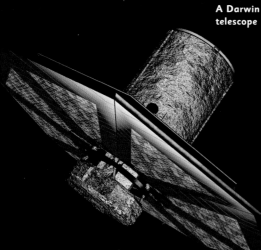

Gliese 581d takes 84 days to orbit its sun and is too cold to support life.

A Darwin telescope

A future eye in space?

The European Space Agency are looking at the possibility of space telescopes that will seek out exoplanets. A flotilla of four telscopes called *Darwin* is planned for launch in 2015. Darwin may not go ahead, as it is just at the planning stage.

Exoplanet HD 189733b was discovered in 2005 as it dimmed the light of its parent star when passing in front of it.

Are there others?

Exoplanets, or extrasolar planets, are planets orbiting a star other than our Sun. More than 200 have been identified since the first was discovered in 1995. Astronomers believe there are many more. Exoplanets cannot be seen through a telescope. One way they are found is by looking for a star's "wobble" as it is affected by an orbiting planet.

Other space telescopes that are looking for planets include Europe's COROT satellite, seen here before launch. It has already detected a planet.

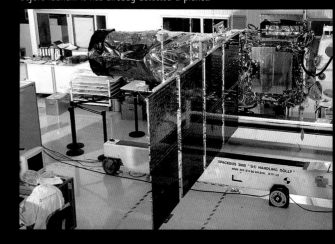

A star is born

Like many space pictures, this image of the Eagle nebula has been artificially coloured so it can be seen clearly.

Clusters of stars are constantly being born from clouds of dust and gas thousands of times the size of our solar system, in a process that can take millions of years.

Born in a cloud

Between existing stars, there are patches of dust and gas. Gradually, these draw in more and more dust and gas to form huge clouds called nebulae. Clumps of matter gather together in these clouds.

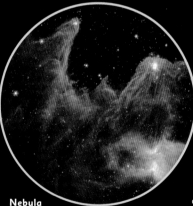

Nebula

Hot colours

As this matter gets more and more dense, heat builds up to form a young star that fills the surrounding nebulae with light and colour. This spectacular effect (right) was captured by the *Spitzer* space telescope.

The process of star formation captured by the *Hubble* telescope.

We have fusion!

With enough matter, this process continues. The star gets denser and hotter. Eventually nuclear fusion begins, releasing huge amounts of heat and light: a star is born.

Which star cluster is also called the Seven Sisters?

What's in a name?

Horsehead, Lagoon, Eagle and Cat's Eye... some of the best-known nebulae have popular names inspired by their shape.

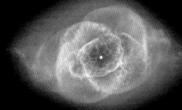

Cat's Eye nebula

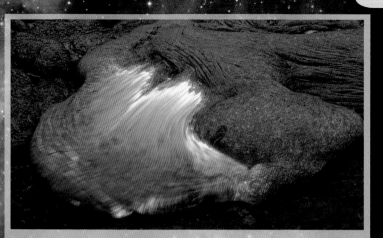

Is that one red?

Some stars shine red, others shine yellow or bluish white. A star's colour depends on its temperature. Red stars are the coolest, while blue stars are the hottest.

In the same way, lava reveals its temperature through its colour. Here, the yellow lava is hotter than the red.

Our Sun is a yellow dwarf star.

What type of star?

Stars have different characteristics according to the amount of matter involved in their birth. They differ in colour, temperature, and brightness, and in the length of time they stay alive.

The life of a star

The Universe is home to lots of different types of star.

Red dwarfs are smaller than our Sun. They burn fuel slowly, so they live a long time.

Young solar systems Leftover material from a star's formation can turn into planets.

Blue giants are among the hottest stars, and live for less than 100 million years.

Supergiants are the rarest stars. They have short lives – under 50 million years.

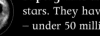

The Pleiades, because you can see seven of its stars without a telescope.

Death of a star

Stars are born, live out their lives, and, ultimately, die. In dying, all their elements are thrown back into the clouds of gas and dust from which they formed, and the process begins again.

Getting bigger...

Moon of planet below

When a star such as our Sun gets old, it begins to expand. It becomes a red giant or supergiant. This is because as it uses up its fuel, hydrogen, its centre or core becomes smaller and hotter. That leads to its expansion.

The surface of a planet whose sky is filled with a red giant star.

Artist's impression of our Sun losing its outer layers at the end of its life.

The moon

weird but true

We are made from elements such as oxygen, hydrogen, carbon, and iron. Hydrogen has been around since time began, while the other elements get made inside stars and spread when they die.

How much longer will our Sun continue to burn its hydrogen?

... and finally smaller

Once it's hot enough, a red giant starts to burn a new fuel called helium. That pushes the outer layers of the star further out. The star then begins to lose these layers as a nebula, and eventually emerges as a small, white dwarf star.

All living things are made from stardust.

Earth

Going out with a bang

Some giant stars end their lives with a huge explosion, called a supernova. Sometimes the centre will survive as a black hole or neutron star.

A giant star pictured before it exploded and formed the supernova 1987a.

1987a: the brightest supernova in Earth's skies for almost four centuries.

A lighthouse in space

Some neutron stars send out radio waves that sweep around as the star spins. Astronomers can pick up these signals. These neutron stars are called pulsars.

Images of dying stars

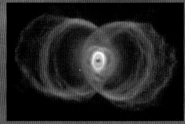
A young hourglass nebula, MyCn18, around a dying star.

An example of a butterfly nebula showing its supersonic "exhaust".

A star's spectacular death in the constellation Taurus, observed as supernova 1054 A.D.

Its fuel will last another five billion years.

Space for everyone

The Sun has set, it's a clear night, and the stars are beginning to appear. Why not go outside and enjoy a bit of astronomy! It's fascinating. It's easy to do. And the more you look, the more you will see.

What do you need?

You don't need special equipment to study the stars: about 2,500 stars are visible to the naked eye, but you will find that binoculars help you to pick out more.

How long does it take your eyes to adjust to the dark?

Constellations
You will soon be spotting constellations. This is a part of the constellation of Sagittarius.

Orion's belt
There are lots of constellations. One of the easiest to pick out is Orion, by spotting the three bright stars that make up this hunter's belt.

Curiosity quiz
Look through the Space for everyone section and see if you can identify the pictures below.

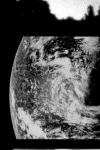

Light pollution
Streetlamps and the light from cars and houses all make the sky brighter, which makes it harder to see. But you can still see the Moon and main constellations. If you are lucky, you may see a comet, or a meteor.

Become an expert...
on stargazing, pages **108-109**
on constellations, pages 112-113

It takes about 30 minutes, especially if you have been in a lit room.

Space for everyone

Basic equipment

Here is a selection of the basic equipment you might find helpful.

Torch

Compass

Torchlight tip
If you need to look at a star map whilst outside, cover the end of your torch in red cellophane. Red light doesn't interfere so much with night sight as white light.

Make notes
It's helpful to note what you have observed. Note the time, year, date, weather conditions, and location. If you can, use a compass, so you know the direction you are looking in.

Binoculars

It's an 8 x 30!
Binoculars are sold in different sizes and powers. The numbers tell you what they are. The first tells you by how many times the binoculars will magnify an object. The second is the measurement in millimeters across the front lenses.

Star maps
It may be worth buying a planisphere. This is a circular map of the stars, made from two plastic discs. Line up the date and time and the discs reveal the stars that can be seen.

Become a stargazer

So you've decided to take a look at the night sky. What will you need to get you going? What should you look for? Here are a few tips to help get you started.

An ancient skill

Astronomy is the study of the Universe. The word "astronomy" comes from two Greek words: *astron*, meaning "star", and *nemein*, meaning "to name".

Larger lenses gather more light, but the larger the lens, the heavier the binoculars.

Holding binoculars steady whilst looking at the night sky can make your arms ache. Try to find something on which you can rest your arms.

Can you name some of the well-known constellations?

Our galaxy, the Milky Way, appears as a burst of stars in a thick band across the night sky.

Light shy

Astronomers prefer to be away from artificial lights and as high as they can get. If you live in a town, see if it's possible to plan a visit to a darker area where you can observe the night sky.

I see a planet!

Look for Venus just after sunset in the western sky or just before sunrise in the eastern sky.

Venus is also known as the morning star, and is always close to the Sun.

The Milky Way is best observed away from towns and cities and the artificial light they create.

Try meteor spotting

The best time to look for meteors is when Earth is passing through meteoroids and a meteor shower is expected. Watch the skies between the 25th July and 18th August when Earth passes through a swarm of meteors called the Perseids. Or try the Orionids between 16th-27th October.

Did you suggest Ursa Major, Leo the lion, or Orion the hunter?

Phases of the moon

Each night over the course of a month, the moon appears to change its shape a little. It doesn't actually do so; what we see is differing amounts of the sunlit side as the moon circles Earth. These shapes are known as phases of the moon, and eight phases make up a complete cycle.

The moon's phases

The complete cycle, from New Moon to Crescent, takes 29.5 days. As the moon appears to grow, it is said to be waxing. As the moon shrinks, it is said to be waning.

8. Waning crescent
The moon has nearly completed a full orbit of Earth. We can only see a sliver.

Sunlight

The moon as it is lit up (or illuminated) in space.

1. New Moon
We cannot see the moon from Earth in this phase, as its lit face is directly towards the Sun.

Sunlight

Scale

If the Earth and moon were the sizes shown here, this would be the distance between them. Earth's gravity has slowed the moon's rotation over billions of years, and now one side permanently faces Earth.

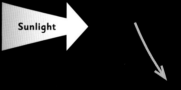

2. Waxing crescent
The moon has moved around a little, and we can see the Sun's light reflecting off part of its surface.

The moon as it appears from Earth.

 We always see the same face of the moon.

What is a blue moon?

7. Last Quarter
The moon has completed three quarters of its orbit around Earth.

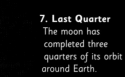

6. Waning gibbous
A sliver of the moon is now no longer visible. The visible part of the moon is waning, or shrinking.

Looking at the phases
This shows the path the moon takes around the Earth, and the moon as it is illuminated in space.

The outer circle shows the moon as it appears from Earth at each stage.

5. Full moon
We can now see the complete face of the moon, reflecting the Sun's light.

4. Waxing gibbous
The moon is showing a little more of itself every night. It is waxing, or growing. "Gibbous" means it looks swollen on one side.

3. First quarter
The moon has completed a quarter of its orbit around Earth.

It's when there are two full moons in the same month.

Constellations

Constellations are collections of stars that can be seen from Earth, and which have been named as groups. This is the space that we can all see and begin to recognize from a very young age.

The celestial sphere

Astronomers once believed that the stars were stuck inside a gigantic globe that enclosed Earth. They named it the celestial sphere. We now know that it doesn't really exist, but it is a helpful way of pinpointing the location of the stars.

How many constellations?

Leo the lion, Orion the hunter... There are 88 internationally recognized constellations. They all have a Latin name, but many have locally known names as well. Each has a story.

Leo the lion is one of the twelve constellations of the zodiac.

Leo the lion

Become an expert...

on the Northern sky, pages 114-115
on the Southern sky, pages 116-117

Can you name some of the signs of the zodiac?

What's the story?

Many constellations were named after characters in ancient Greek myth. Orion was named because ancient astronomers imagined two lines of stars picked out this hunter's belt and sword.

Orion

The zodiac

This is an imaginary band within which the Sun, moon, and planets appear to travel. The 12 constellations, or signs of the zodiac, that lie on this band are seen as special by astrologers.

The twelve signs of the zodiac lie on an imaginary band in the sky.

Close neighbours

A constellation's stars are not as close together as they appear. This diagram of the Cassiopeia constellation shows how the distances vary.

Are you north or south?

The sphere of the sky is divided into two halves: the northern and southern celestial hemispheres. Which stars and constellations you can see depends on where you live on the Earth.

The closest star in the Cassiopeia constellation is just over 50 light years away. The most distant is more than 600 light years away.

Leo, Scorpio, Cancer, Aries, Gemini, and Pisces are six of the 12 signs.

The northern sky

This star map shows some of the constellations in the northern hemisphere (that's anywhere north of the equator). Choose a clear night and look up. If you live near the equator, you won't be able to spot all these stars all year.

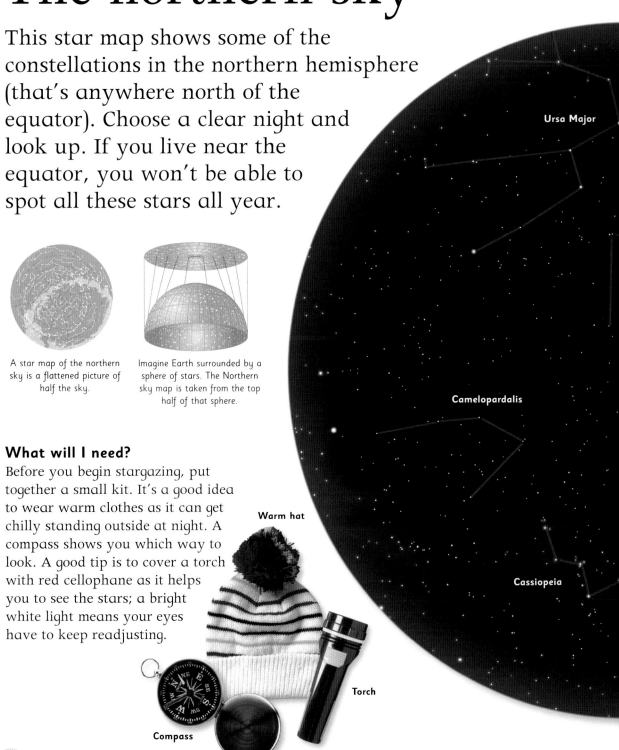

A star map of the northern sky is a flattened picture of half the sky.

Imagine Earth surrounded by a sphere of stars. The Northern sky map is taken from the top half of that sphere.

Ursa Major

Camelopardalis

Cassiopeia

Warm hat

Torch

Compass

What will I need?

Before you begin stargazing, put together a small kit. It's a good idea to wear warm clothes as it can get chilly standing outside at night. A compass shows you which way to look. A good tip is to cover a torch with red cellophane as it helps you to see the stars; a bright white light means your eyes have to keep readjusting.

Which distinctive constellation is used as a "signpost" in the nouthern sky?

Start spotting the constellations

You'll find it soon becomes easy to pick out more constellations than those shown. Some, such as the well-known hunter Orion, are visible in both Northern and Southern skies.

The Great Bear

Ursa Major (the Great Bear) is supposed to represent Callisto, a beautiful girl who was turned into a bear by Zeus's wife (Zeus was the king of the gods).

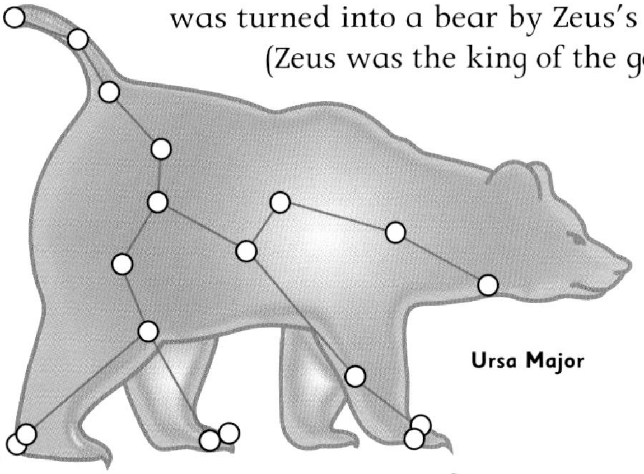

Draco

Ursa Minor

Cepheus

Ursa Major

Cameleopardalis

This constellation was only named some 400 years ago – that's relatively recent for a constellation. It represents a giraffe.

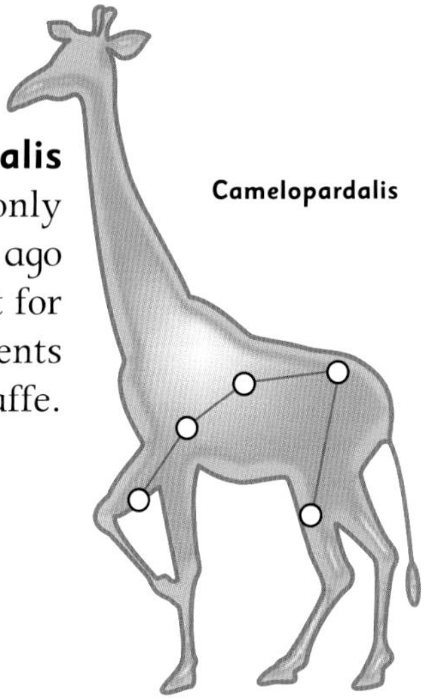

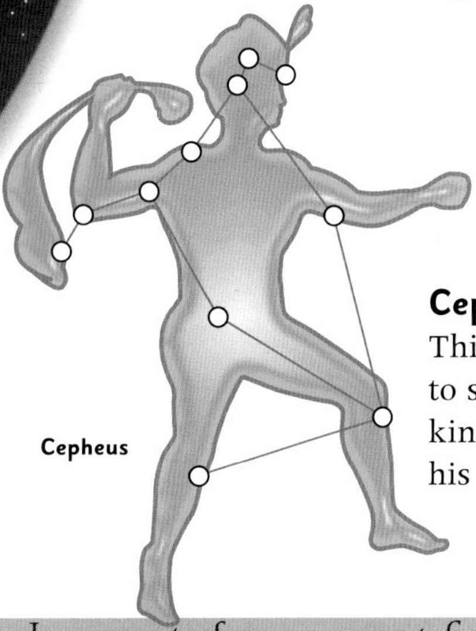

Cameleopardalis

Cepheus

This constellation is said to show a mythical Greek king, who stands next to his wife, Cassiopeia.

Cepheus

The southern sky

This star map shows some of the constellations in the southern hemisphere (that's anywhere south of the equator). Choose a clear night and look up. If you live near the equator, you won't be able to spot all these stars all year.

A star map of the southern sky is a flattened picture of half the sky.

Imagine Earth surrounded by a sphere of stars. The southern sky map is taken from the bottom half of that sphere.

They won't stay still!

As you begin star spotting you will notice that the stars and constellations don't appear to be fixed in the same place. This is because the Earth's rotation makes the stars appear to move.

The stars' apparent movement shows clearly on a long exposure photograph of the night sky.

Centaurus

Pavo

Which distinctive constellation is used as a "signpost" in the southern sky?

Spotting the constellations

The more stargazing you do, the easier it becomes to pick out constellations. Here are a few that you can look for in southern skies.

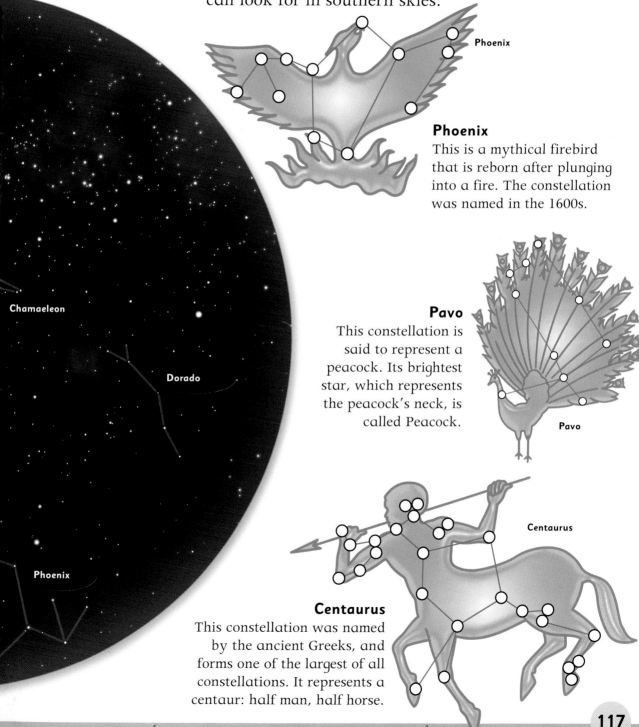

Phoenix

This is a mythical firebird that is reborn after plunging into a fire. The constellation was named in the 1600s.

Pavo

This constellation is said to represent a peacock. Its brightest star, which represents the peacock's neck, is called Peacock.

Centaurus

This constellation was named by the ancient Greeks, and forms one of the largest of all constellations. It represents a centaur: half man, half horse.

Chamaeleon

Dorado

Phoenix

Space technology

Some of the inventions we use today are closely connected to the space program. Just take a look at the following.

A hand-held Dustbuster has super-suction power.

Cordless tools

Space scientists and power-tool designers together made cordless tools so astronauts could drill rock on the moon. This work led to the invention of cordless medical instruments and a cordless vacuum cleaner.

Surgeons use lightweight, battery-powered instruments.

Medical scans

Computer technology, designed to enhance pictures of the moon, is used by medical staff. It makes scans of the human body easy to read so doctors can diagnose disease.

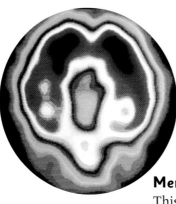

Scan of a human head

Memory foam

This was developed to improve seating and crash protection for pilots. The foam moulds to the shape of the body, then returns to its original shape.

Memory foam is used here in a neck cushion.

What is "memory foam" also known as?

Aerodynamic bicycle wheel

Following research, three-spoked bicycle wheels were developed into shapes that move quickly and easily.

These wheels maximize the bikes' efficiency for racing.

Material facts

Some people believe these materials were invented for the space program, when in fact they were just used by it. The heat-resistant plastic, Teflon, for example, was invented in 1938 and later used on space suits and heat shields.

Teflon is commonly used as a non-stick covering for cooking pans. It is also a stain resistant fabric protector.

Velcro was used during the Apollo missions to hold equipment in place at zero gravity, when it would otherwise have floated off. Velcro is also used to secure clothing.

Things like these

During the 1960s onwards, US space agency NASA adapted everyday objects for use in its space program.

NASA made its own smoke detector with adjustable sensitivity. It also used smoke detectors on Skylab, the space station launched in 1973, to detect toxic vapours.

ISBN 1-4053-1037

9 781405 31037

A type of bar coding was used by NASA to keep track of spacecraft components.

Quartz clocks were first used in the 1920s. In the 1960s, NASA worked to produce a highly accurate quartz clock.

Space timeline

Since humankind began exploring space in the 1950s, there have been a number of key moments. From the first satellite to the launch of the first space station, take a look at some of these amazing events.

Sputnik

1957
The first man-made satellite, *Sputnik 1*, took approximately 98 minutes to orbit Earth.

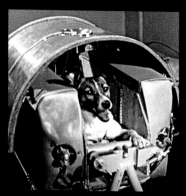

1957
The first living creature was sent into space: Laika the dog was strapped into *Sputnik 2*.

Luna 3 was a Soviet spacecraft.

1959
We had our first glimpse of the far side of the moon from the Luna 3 spacecraft.

1961
The first human in space: Yuri Gagarin's orbit of Earth lasted 108 minutes.

1963
The first woman in space: Valentina Tereshkova on Vostok 6. The flight lasted 70 hours, 50 minutes and orbited Earth 48 times.

1965
The first space walk, lasting about 10 minutes, was achieved by Alexei Arkhipovich Leonov.

1969
The first human to step on the moon was Neil Armstrong from Apollo 11. The other crew member who walked on the moon was Edward "Buzz" Aldrin.

Astronaut Buzz Aldrin walks on the moon.

What was the name of the third astronaut on the *Apollo 11* mission?

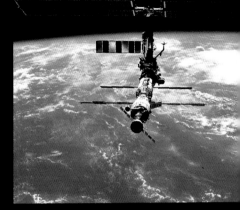

The International Space Station

1973

The first US space station, *Skylab*, went into orbit. It was to be manned by three successive crews who would perform nearly 300 experiments whilst on board. *Skylab* fell back to Earth in 1979.

1977

Voyager 2 is launched, closely followed by *Voyager 1*. The spacecraft have studied the solar system's outer planetary systems, and are still operating.

1986

The first section of *Mir*, the Russian space station, was launched. *Mir* was the first permanent residence in space and was almost continuously occupied until 1999. *Mir* burnt up in Earth's atmosphere, after 15 years in orbit, in 2001.

Lift off of *Titan III-Centaur* vehicle carrying *Voyager 2*.

1998

The first part of the International Space Station (ISS) was launched. Still in operation today, it is powered by large solar panels and orbits the Earth at an altitude of 360 kms (225 miles).

2004

Cassini reached Saturn and sent back the clearest photographs ever of Saturn's ring system. The image below shows the rings and their shadow on the planet Saturn.

Mir space station

Cassini image of Saturn's rings.

Glossary

Asteroid A minor planet, actually just a giant rock, usually one that circles the Sun. There are hundreds of thousands in our solar system and more are being discovered all the time.

Astronaut A person who has been trained to travel inside a spacecraft.

Astronomy The branch of science that studies the places beyond Earth such as stars, planets, comets, and galaxies.

Atmosphere The thin layer of gas surrounding the Earth for about 100 km (63 miles) which fades gradually into space beyond.

Black hole An area with a gravitational pull so strong that it sucks in anything that comes too close.

Scientists know black holes exist because of their effect on nearby stars.

Comet A space snowball made of dust, rock, and ice that orbits the Sun. Comets have tails when near the Sun.

Galaxy A large system of stars, gas, dust, and empty space that rotates but is held together by gravity. Earth and its solar system are part of a galaxy called the Milky Way.

Gas Freely moving atoms or particles without a definite shape.

Gravity The attraction between everything in the Universe. Gravity makes Earth and the other planets in the solar system orbit the Sun, and the moon rotate around Earth.

Light year The distance light travels in one year.

Meteor A piece of rock or dust that burns up as it enters Earth's atmosphere.

Meteorite A meteor that hits the Earth without being destroyed.

Moon A natural satellite – an object orbiting a planet. Earth has one moon, though there are hundreds in our solar system.

Nebula A cloud of dust and gas in space that may eventually give birth to stars.

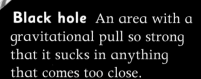

Observatory Any place used to look into space. Optical observatories have a dome, often in a high-up location, housing a telescope. The roof can be opened to look at the sky. There are also radio observatories with big dishes, and space-based observatories – telescopes floating in space.

Orbit The path an object makes around another object while under the influence of gravity.

Planet A large, round object orbiting a star.

Rocket Rockets carry satellites and people into space.

Satellite An object that orbits something larger than itself. The moon is a natural satellite. Artificial satellites are objects put in orbit by humans.

Solar system The planets, moons, dwarf planets, comets, asteroids, and dust that orbit the Sun, held by its gravity.

Space The huge, largely empty areas in between the atmospheres of stars and planets. Space contains dust, gas, and the odd rock.

Spacecraft A vehicle or device designed to travel in space.

Space shuttle The system used by the US government for its human space-flight missions. The orbiter, which carries the astronauts, can be reused.

Space station A space laboratory orbiting the Earth operated by crews of astronauts who live there for weeks or months.

Star A self-heating ball of glowing gas.

Sun The star nearest to the Earth. It powers life on Earth.

Telescope An instrument used to look at very distant things.

UFO Unidentified flying objects are objects in the sky that people claim to have seen but cannot be identified. Some people cite them as evidence of life beyond Earth.

Universe Everything! The Earth and its moon, the Sun, the planets of the solar system, and all the galaxies – even things we haven't yet discovered.

Index

A

air 7, 35
Aldrin, Buzz 34, 120
aliens 89, 92
Alpha Centauri 21
Apollo 11 spacecraft 32-33, 34, 35, 120
Ares 1 rocket launcher 37
Ariane 5 rocket 30-31
Armstrong, Neil 33, 34, 35, 120
asteroid 14, 50, 74-75, 77, 82-83, 84-85
    Eros 84-85
    Itokawa 84
asteroid belt 50, 82-83
astronaut 4, 5, 24, 26-27, 28-29, 32, 33, 39, 40-41, 42-43, 99
astronomy 8, 106-118
Atlantis shuttle and orbiter 6, 37
atmosphere 6, 21, 35, 60, 64, 66, 72

B

ar codes 119
Barnard's Star 48
bicycle wheels 119
Big Bang 88, 96-97
black hole 11, 98-99

C

allisto (Jupiter's moon) 50, 68-69
Camelopardalis 115
Cassini orbiter 121
Cassini-Huygens orbiter-probe 25, 71
Celestial sphere 112
Centaurus 117
Cepheus 115
Ceres 74-5, 83
Challenger orbiter 37, 87
Chandra telescope 11
Charon (Pluto's moon) 75
clothes 28, 29
Collins, Mike 34
Columbia orbiter 37
comet 14, 50, 56, 76-87
command module 32, 33, 34
constellations 106, 112-117
Copernicus 8

cordless tools 118
COROT satellite 101
cosmonaut 24, 30
Crew Exploration Vehicle (CEV) 37
crop circles 90

D

aedalus 48
dark matter 23
Darwin telescope 101
Deimos (Mars's moon) 64
Discovery orbiter 37
dust 4, 14, 50, 64, 102
dwarf planet 14, 74-75, 83
dwarf star 21, 103

E

arth 5, 6, 8, 14-15, 22, 34, 35, 50, 51, 53, 60-61, 62-63, 64, 66, 74, 87, 110
escape velocity 31
Extravehicular Mobility Unit (EMU) 28, 29
Endeavour orbiter 37
Enterprise spacecraft 49
Eros asteroid 84-85
Europa (Jupiter's moon) 50, 68-69
exoplanets 101
exosphere 6

F

airing 7, 30
fuel tank 7, 31, 36

G

agarin, Yuri 30, 120
Gaia satellite 7
galaxy 15, 16-17, 22, 97
Galilei, Galileo 8, 67, 68

Galileo telescope 67, 82, 83

Ganymede (Jupiter's moon) 50, 68-69

gas 4, 6, 14, 30, 60, 66, 72, 102

Gliese 581 star 100

gravity 4, 31, 40, 63, 82, 98, 99, 110

gravity assists 25

Great Dark Spot 73

Great Red Spot 66

Halley's comet 78
Hayabusa 84
Helios 2 49
Hubble telescope 9
Hydra (Pluto's moon) 75

International Space Station 29, 38, 42, 121
interstellar travel 48-49
Io (Jupiter's moon) 50, 67, 68-69
Itokawa asteroid 84

James Webb telescope 9
Jupiter 14, 50, 66-67, 68-69, 76

Keck telescope 10

Laika the dog 120
Leo 112
Leonids 81

Leonov, Alexei 43, 120

light year 4, 19, 20

Local Group 15, 16

Long March 2C rocket 30

Luna 3 probe 63, 120

Luna 9 probe 63

lunar module 32, 33

Lunar Prospector 63

lunar rover 34

Magellan probe 59
Mariner 10 probe 56
Marius, Simon 68, 69
Mars 14, 46-47, 50, 64-65, 94-95
Mars Global Surveyor 46
Mars Polar Lander 46
Mars rovers 46, 47

medical instruments 118

Mercury 14, 50, 56-57, 61

mesosphere 6

Messenger probe 57

meteor 14, 56, 63, 76-87, 109

meteorite 77, 80

Milky Way 15, 16, 18-19, 22, 109

Mir space station 6, 38, 121

Miranda (Uranus's moon) 73

moons
    Earth's moon 8, 14, 32-33, 34-35, 44, 49, 54, 55, 62-63, 74, 107, 110-111, 120
    Jupiter's moons 50, 67, 68-69
    Mars's moons 64
    Neptune's moons 73
    Pluto's moons 75
    Saturn's moons 71
    Uranus's moons 73

multiverse 23

N ASA 7, 26, 27, 37
NEAR-*Shoemaker* probe 84-85
nebula 4, 88, 102
Neptune 14, 50-51, 72, 73
Nix (Pluto's moon) 75
northern hemisphere 113, 114-115
nose cone 7, 30

O bservatories 10-11, 95
Opportunity rover 47
orbiter 7, 36
Atlantis 6, 37
Challenger 37, 87
Columbia 37
Discovery 37
Endeavour 37
Orion 112, 113, 115
Orion CEV 37
Orion's belt 106

P athfinder spacecraft 46
Pavo 117
payload 31
payload bay 26, 37
Perseids 109
Phobos (Mars's moon) 64
Phoenix 117
Pioneer probe 93
Pluto 14, 50, 51, 57, 74-75
probes
Daedelus 48
Huygens 25, 71
Luna 3 63, 120
Luna 9 63
Lunar Prospector 63
Magellan 59
Mariner 10 56
Messenger 57
NEAR-*Shoemaker* 84-85
Pioneer 93
SOHO 52
TRACE 52
Ulysses 52
Promixa Centauri 20, 21, 49
"pumpkin suit" 28

R adio telescope 12-13, 92-93
radio waves 12, 13
rocket 4, 30-31
Ariane 5 30-31
Long March 2C 30
Saturn V 31, 32
Vostock 1 30
rocket booster 7, 36
rocket launcher 37
Roswell 91
rovers
Opportunity 47
Sojourner 46
Spirit 46-47

S agittarius 106
Salyut space station 38
satellite 4, 7, 14, 29, 30, 31, 44-45, 51, 62, 120, 121
COROT 101
Gaia 7
Sputnik 45, 120
Telstar 44
Saturn 14, 25, 50-51, 70-71
Saturn V rocket 31, 32
service module 32, 33, 34
shooting stars 80-81
shuttle 6, 7, 29, 31, 36-37
Atlantis 6, 37
Skylab space station 38, 121
SOHO probe 52
Sojourner rover 46
solar eclipse 54-55
solar system 14, 22, 50-75, 82-83
solar wind 52
Sojourner probe 46
southern hemisphere 113, 116-117
Soyuz space station 39
space probe 52, 56, 57, 63, 71, 84, 85, 93

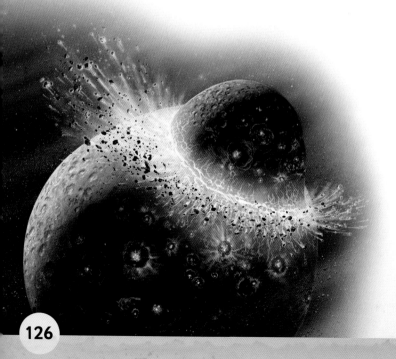

space station 6, 29, 38-39, 120, 121
  Mir 6, 38, 121
  Salyut 38
  Skylab 38, 121
  Soyuz 39
spacecraft 7, 24-25, 48, 71
  Apollo 11 32-33, 34, 35, 120
  Enterprise 49
  Galileo 67, 82, 83
  Hayabusa 84
  Helios 2 49
  Mars 2 46
  Mars 3 46
  Pathfinder 46
  Voyager 1 22, 24, 68, 93
  Voyager 2 73, 93, 121
spacewalk 42, 43
Spirit rover 46-47
Spitzer telescope 4, 102
Sputnik satellite 45, 120
stars 4, 11, 18, 20-21, 22, 52, 88, 97, 98, 100, 102-103, 104-105
stratosphere 6
Sun 4, 8, 14, 20, 22, 45, 50, 52-53, 54-55, 56, 58, 60, 66, 67, 72, 82, 97, 103
sunspot 52
supernova 88, 105

Teflon 119
telescope 8-9, 10-11, 12-13, 18, 88, 92-93, 99, 101
  Chandra 11
  Hubble 9
  James Webb 9
  Keck 10
  radio 12-13, 92-93
  Spitzer 4
  Telstar satellite 44
Tereshkova, Valentina 120
thermosphere 6
Titan (Saturn's moon) 71

Titania (Uranus's moon) 73
TRACE probe 52
Triton (Neptune's moon) 73
troposphere 6

UFOs 89, 90-91
Ulysses probe 52
Universe 4, 8, 14, 22-23, 96-97
Uranus 14, 50-51, 72, 73
Ursa Major (Great Bear) 115

Velcro 119
Venus 14, 50, 58-59, 61, 109
Viking landers 46
Viking Orbiter 1 65
volcano 10, 46, 59, 65
Vostok 1 rocket 30
Voyager 1 spacecraft 22, 24, 68, 93, 121
Voyager 2 spacecraft 73, 93, 121

Weightlessness 4, 27
White, Edward 43

Zodiac 113

Picture credits

The publisher would like to thank the following for their kind permission to reproduce their photographs:

(Key: a-above; b-below/bottom; c-centre; l-left; r-right; t-top)

Alamy Images: eStock Photo 56cla, 58tl, 64tl, 66tr, 70tr, 72tr, 75ca; Rab Harling 91bl; TNT Magazine 89cr; Richard Wainscoat 10-11b. **Bridgeman Art Library**: Victoria Art Gallery, Bath and North East Somerset Council 94cl. **Corbis**: 6bl, 19br, 35br, 35tc, 125b; Neil Armstrong 34 (Buzz Aldrin); Hinrich Baesemann/epa 52cl; Heide Benser 118cr; Bettmann 8cla, 25fcr, 28br, 33cb, 35clb, 35tr, 91br, 91cr; Bettmann/Neil Armstrong 34c; Bettmann/Paul Trent 90-91cb; Paul Chinn/San Francisco Chronicle 90cl; Richard Cummins 49t; Tim De Waele 119tr; ESA/NASA 38-39c; Firefly Productions 11tl; Tim Kiusalaas 60cla; NASA 18tr, 60bl, 67tc, 110bl, 123br; NASA TV/epa 29b; NASA TV/Handout/epa 39cr; NASA/epa 37cra; NASA/JPL-Caltech 52br; NASA/Roger Ressmeyer 18bl, 29tc; Roger Ressmeyer 77br (mission control), 87b, 107fcrb, 113tr, 118crb; Reuters 11tr, 38bl, 67cr; John Sevigny/epa 70b; Jim Sugar 61cr. **DK Images**: Science Museum, London 8bl, 86tr, 118ftl; NASA 7bl, 44, 53tc, 69cb, 77clb (comet), 99cb, 99clb, 99cr, 101tl, 121ftl; NASA/Finley Holiday Films 68 (jupiter); NASA/JPL 51br, 66cl; Natural History Museum, London 80tl. **European Space Agency**: 7br, 9br, 31cr, 51cla, 101bl, 101tr; Studio - Bazile 101br. **Getty Images**: LWA 5tr, 19l; Riser/ Sightseeing Archive 34br; Antonio M Rosario 18cr; Space Frontiers/Dera 60-61c; Time & Life Pictures 121b. **JAXA**: ISAS 77crb (Itokawa), 84b, 84clb. **David Malin Images**: UK Schmidt Telescope/ DSS/AAO 21r. **Mary Evans Picture Library**: 8l, 95tr. **NASA**: 1r, 4b, 4cl, 4cla, 4clb, 5bl, 6-7, 24br, 24fbr, 25br, 25fcra, 25fcrb, 25ftr, 26bl, 27b, 27r, 27tr, 28cb, 28clb, 28crb, 29tl (liferaft), 30ca, 31l, 31tr, 32tl, 36clb, 36r, 37br, 37cl, 37tl, 38cl, 39tl, 40cl, 40-41 (running machine), 41br, 41cla, 41clb, 41tr, 42tr, 42-43, 43b, 43cr, 43tr, 45bc, 45bl, 45c, 45ca, 45clb, 45crb, 45fclb, 45tr, 46br (polar lander), 46cr, 46cra (viking lander), 46crb, 46tl, 46-47 (b/g), 46-47b, 47cla, 47ftr, 47tr, 51fbr, 51tc, 51tl, 52bl, 52clb, 52fclb, 55br, 59tr, 64-65c, 68cr, 68ftr, 68tr, 69bc, 69ca, 69crb, 69l, 69tc, 69tc (false colour), 71tr, 72br, 72r, 73bc, 73bl, 73br, 73c, 73cla, 73clb, 73tr, 75br, 75cb, 77clb (asteroid), 77clb (meteorite), 79b, 83bc, 83cb, 88bc, 89cla, 89tr, 90cr, 93c, 93cr, 93cra, 102cl, 103cra, 103crb (yellow dwarf), 105cl, 105cr, 120tr, 124tl, 127, 128; ESA, H. Weaver-JHU/APL, A. Stern-SwRI/HST Pluto Companion Search Team 75tr; ESA, K. Noll-STScI/ Hubble Heritage Team (STScI/ AURA) 8-9t; GSFC 98c, 105fcr, 105fcra; H. Hammel, MIT 76bl; HQ-GRIN 89cr, 89fbr, 102br; JHUAPL/ Carnegie Institution of Washington 57bl; JPL 85ftr, 85tc, 85tr, 105fcrb; JSC 121tl; MSFC 84tl, 99tc, 103br (supergiant), 121ca, 121tr; D. Roddy (U.S. Geological Survey), Lunar and Planetary Institute 81cla (meteor crater). **National Radio Astronomy Observatory**: AUI/Dave Finley 13tl. **PunchStock**: Digital Archive Japan 52tl. **Science Photo Library**: 68bl, 71clb, 96tl; Mike Agliolo 78tl; David P. Anderson/SMU/NASA 58-59b; Julian Baum 42cra, 67bc, 76-77; Julian Baum/New Scientist 88-89; Sally Bensusen 54br; BMDO/NRL/LLNL 51fcra, 63bl; Peter Bowater 45tl; Chris Butler 56-57b, 70cl, 74cl, 89cra, 104-105c; Celestial Image Co. 14br, 112l, 113r; China Great Wall Industry Corporation 30b; John Chumack 77tr, 79cr; Lynette Cook 82bl, 126bl; David Ducros 24-25; Bernhard Edmaier 77cra, 80bc; Hermann Eisenbeiss 62tr; Dr. Fred Espenak 12b, 54c, 109br; European Southern Observatory 100; European Space Agency 64cla, 71cb, 89br, 98bl; European Space Agency/ DLR/FU Berlin/G. Neukum 65tr; John Foster 80-81; Mark Garlick 14tl, 19tr, 21b, 48-49b, 49cl, 74br, 74-75, 82-83c, 83tl, 96-97; Robert Gendler 14clb; David A. Hardy 25bl, 48clb; David A. Hardy, Futures: 50 Years In Space 16-17, 104-105 (b/g); Adam Hart-Davis 47cr; Johns Hopkins University Applied Physics Laboratory 84-85cb; JPL-Caltech/STSCI/Vassar/NASA 5br, 14-15t; Manfred Kage 81clb (meteorite fragment); Mehau Kulyk 23br, 86bl, 98-99cb; Larry Landolfi 4c, 51ca, 62-63; Dr. Michael J. Ledlow 57tr; G. Brad Lewis 103tl; Library Of Congress 95crb; Lockheed Martin Corporation/NASA 2-3; Jerry Lodriguss 21t, 77tc, 78-79, 106fbl, 107cl; Jean Lorre 64clb; Andrew J. Martinez 63ca, 63cra; Max-Planck Institute for Radio Astronomy 12l; Robert Mcnaught 78cl; Peter Menzel 13br; Allan Morton/Dennis Milon 16cla, 109t; MSSS/JPL/NASA 51fcrb, 65cr; David Nanuk 10l, 13l; NASA 26r, 37cr, 38fclb, 46clb, 55cra, 64bl, 66-67c, 87tl, 107fcra, 111cl, 120br, 122; NASA/ESA/ STSCI/ Hubble Heritage Team 65bc; NASA/JPL/Space Science Institute 107fbr, 121crb; National Optical Astronomy Observatories 102-103; David Nunuk 5cra, 12c; Walter Pacholka-Astropics 80ca; David Parker 11r, 92c; David Parker-ESA/CNES/Arianespace 31bc; Physics Today Collection/ American Institute of Physics 97cr; George Post 55l; Ria Novosti 30clb, 38clb, 43cla, 120bl, 120cr (moon), 120fcla, 120fclb; Paul Robbens & Gus York 33br; Royal Observatory, Edinburgh 15bl; Royal Observatory, Edinburgh/AAO 5crb (nebula); John Sanford 28-29t, 107tc, 110-111 (moons), 111fbr; Friedrich Saurer 13bl, 15tr, 34tr, 36bl, 40cb, 42bl, 48c, 56cb, 64ca, 67tr, 81cra, 91tc, 97br, 104cb, 111ftr; Jerry Schad 106-107 (b/g), 107ftr, 109c; K. Sharon/Tel Aviv U./NASA/ESA/STSCI 22-23c; Dr Seth Shostak 89crb, 92-93c; Eckhard Slawik 107tl; SOHO/ESA/NASA 51ftr, 53c; Sheila Terry 78bl; US Geological Survey 56-57, 65fcrb; Detlev Van Ravenswaay 5cr, 20-21l, 50-51, 51fcr, 65cb, 70-71, 81tr, 83cra; Victor Habbick Visions 90-91tc, 94-95; Richard J. Wainscoat, Peter Arnold Inc. 78br; F. Winkler, Middlebury College, MCELS Team/NOAO/ AURA/NSF 15br; Frank Zullo 116bl. **Still Pictures**: Astrofoto 95bl. **STScI**: J. Bedke 9tr. **TopFoto.co.uk**: 94clb; Fortean 90bl; Ria Novosti 120clb.

All other images © Dorling Kindersley
For further information see: www.dkimages.com

Acknowledgements

Dorling Kindersley would like to thank:
Jon Woodcock for his invaluable guidance, patience, and humour; Peter Bull for artworks; Hedi Gutt and Clare Harris for design assistance; Fleur Star for compiling the index; and Alex Cox, Deborah Lock, and Zahavit Shalev for editorial assistance.

An astronaut in an extravehicular mobility unit (an EMU). Learn more about these spacesuits on page 28.